FACEBOOK ADVERTISING 2020:

THE ULTIMATE BEGINNERS GUIDE WITH THE LATEST STRATEGIES ON HOW TO BECOME A TOP INFLUENCER EVEN IF YOU HAVE A SMALL BUSINESS (SOCIAL MEDIA MASTERY ADS GUIDE)

Table of Contents

Conclusion

Description

Whether you are just starting or established your business ten years ago, you will be able to grow your business with Facebook. If you haven't created your Facebook business page, this is your first step. From there, you can create advertisements following your schedule and budget. By paying attention to your customers' needs and wants, you will be able to develop some of the most engaging advertisements for your target audience.

Creating an ideal customer profile is an important step when you are determining your target audience. Through your ideal customer, you can get an idea of their age range, location, gender, and interests. Once your advertisements are up and running, you will be able to use Facebook's analytics in order to improve your ideal customer profile. This will only help you increase engagement and customers.

Once you have your ideal customer in place, you will want to create a detailed marketing plan. This plan will include everything from your mission to your customer service support.

This book is created as a guide that you can read and reread. It will be helpful as you start to grow your customer base through Facebook. You can turn to the pages of this book when you are looking for your next advertising strategy, such as PPC or Facebook Messenger Ads. If you are unsure of your next step, you can look through this book as it will help you reach your next step.

Your dedication, patience, will to succeed and this valuable information are going to take you farther than you thought possible in the Facebook advertising market. No matter how prepared you are to integrate the words of this book into your Facebook advertising, you want to remember that it all takes time. No success happens overnight. Whether your business is one year old or twenty, it will take time for Facebook users to start noticing your business and advertising. Don't let this discourage you. Instead, remember success comes to those who are patient and dedicated.

This guide will focus on the following:

- The Importance of a Facebook Page
- Choosing Your Audience
- Choose & refine your page theme
- Using advertising functions on Facebook
- Making Ads - Targeting
- Avoid being banned from advertising on Facebook
- Content Marketing in Facebook
- Facebook Sales Funnel
- How to Set up Facebook Business Manager
- Choose The Best Advertising Option For Your Business on Facebook
- How To Use Facebook Like A Pro For Your Business
- Psychology Behind Ads
- AdWords vs. Facebook… AND MORE!!!

Introduction

This chapter assumes that you haven't set up a Facebook for your business already. If you have, it's still worth your time to give it a glance for some basic design tips. If you're reading this and have already set up a personal page on Facebook, be aware that business pages aren't as simple to establish, though they do function more or less the same. Regardless, it's important to follow this guide as you set up the page because not every step is self-explanatory.

To begin you'll first go to Facebook.com. If you aren't logged into your personal account then to the right you'll see the first stages for setting up a personal account. Beneath the fields asking for your first and last name, mobile number and other personal information, you'll see the "Create Account" button. Below that is the link to create a page. Click that link to begin. If you are logged in you'll automatically be taken to your news feed instead. Click the downward arrow in the upper right-hand corner (the rightmost button in the blue bar at the top) and click "Create Page" from the drop-down menu.

Note: you're going to need a personal page in order to set-up an account. If you aren't logged in when you go to set up your business page you'll be prompted later in the process to log in to continue. If you don't have a personal Facebook page you must set one up before establishing a business page; you won't be permitted to make a business page without one. If you haven't set up a personal page already, go to Facebook.com and follow the onscreen instructions.

When setting up a business page you're first presented with six categories: local business or place; company, organization or institution; brand or product; artist, band or public figure; entertainment; and cause or community. Pick the one that best describes what you're marketing and click on its tile. When you do it changes into a registration field. Each one varies slightly but they all require a name. Each selection also has a drop-down list of categories (except for cause and community). If you're still unsure which page type you fall under, browse through each list of categories.

The importance of selecting the right page type cannot be overstated. Though they may seem outwardly similar, they display different information. The most in-depth are local business/place and company/organization/institution, which allow for addresses for physical storefronts and offices, telephone numbers for direct contact, website addresses, a display showing your business address on a map, and allow for users to leave reviews and to share with other Facebook users when they check in. When running a business with an offline counterpart these two page types are your best options. Enter the required information and continue. That said, you're allowed to change your page's category any number of times you want once it's been established. The only consequence to this is that you'll lose any features unique to your previous category.

At this point you'll be prompted to log in to your personal account to continue if you aren't logged in already. This is necessary for account management.

The next screen is divided into five tabs. The first is "About." You're allowed to enter up to two more categories next to the one you've already selected. Start typing a word that describes what you're marketing and Facebook will make suggestions based on that. You have to use these suggestions; you cannot enter your own categories. It's in your best interest to have three categories to improve your standing in search results for Facebook users. You can then enter a brief description of your page (which you will expand on later) and a web address for a corresponding preexisting website. The next step is choosing your Facebook URL (what follows "www.facebook.com/" to bring users to your page). You have total freedom of what this part of the address is, but if it already exists you'll have to modify it. Pick a name that corresponds to what you're marketing. Finally, depending on the categories, you"ll be asked if this is a real establishment or venue. Checking "yes" on these selections results in Facebook asking if you're the owner or have the authority to make the page. Follow the onscreen instructions for verification.

Tab two is where you select your profile picture. Like with your personal account, this image will appear at the top of your new page and beside each post you make with it. Try to pick something that represents the business or product you're selling. If you have a physical location a nice photo of the inside or outside of the building is an easy choice. If you have a logo that also makes for a good profile image. Just remember, though, the image is relatively small, so don't use an image crammed with text. If you're coming up short you can always hire a freelance designer or photographer to make the image for you.

"Add to Favorites" is the third and least consequential tab. It will allow you to add the business page to your favorites on your personal profile. A link will appear on the left-hand side of the screen whenever you're logged in to your personal account, allowing you to switch over to and manage your business page with a single click.

The fourth tab (which may not appear) is "Claim." This happens when there are multiple pages with the same name. The purpose of this page is to merge preexisting duplicate profile pages. There may already be a generic listing for your business if other users have listed it as something they like or as a favorite in their profile. Claim these pages if they represent your business; this will merge the duplicate page into the one you're making. If your business has a generic or common name it's likely that it will show other pages that aren't duplicates or are generic placeholders. Don't claim these—they belong to someone else!

The last tab is some basic advertising info that will help your page appear in front of your target demographics based on location, age range, gender, language and interests. While this stage is important it doesn't have impact on paid ads should you choose to make them. Instead it will determine which demographics your page will show up for as a page users within those parameters might like based on their interests and Facebook activity.

When you've completed these last steps you will be taken to your page which, at this stage, is noticeably empty. You can go about filling the missing information right away, but be aware that your page is automatically in a published state, making it entirely visible to other users. If you want to change this click "Settings" in the upper right-hand corner and under "General" toggle page visibility to unpublished. Return to this page when you're ready to go live. If you're planning on filling out the page right away there's no real need to unpublish it.

When filling out your page there are three important things that need to be addressed right away:

Edit Page Info—This section allows you to fill out a massive amount of information regarding your business, service or product based on the category you selected. Some of this is automatically filled out based on what you entered during the previous setup steps. Others are entirely optional and may not apply to you. That being the case, it's good practice to fill out as many relevant sections as you can. Doing so will give your page a professional outward appearance. All this information will be found by visitors when they click "About" on your page. It's important to give new visitors as much info upfront as you can to help guide them through what you do and what you're marketing.

Cover Image—You'll know this from your personal page. The cover image is a massive banner that appears at the top of your page and beside your profile image. It's meant to compliment your profile image but will appear in less places than your profile image. It plays the role of creating a strong first impression when users land on your page. Apply the same considerations we outlined from your profile image to your cover image. Make sure it's visually pleasant when combined with the rest of the page. Again, it's worth your time to get the opinions of others in this regard, and consult a professional or freelance designer if you're unsure. There are many free templates you can use online to design a cover photo, too.

Call To Action Button—A button that appears near the top of your page that can be programmed to take customers to other pages, be it your About page or a storefront on your website. The seven categories are fairly self-explanatory, so choose the one that is most appropriate for your business. When editing the button you'll pick a category ("Contact Us" or "Shop Now," for example) and add a hyperlink that the button will direct customers to when they click. The CTA button helps direct people to your main goal while also making a public statement about what your ultimate goal is.

You're almost ready to begin marketing in earnest, but click around if you want to make yourself familiar with some of the features available to you (don't worry, we'll be going over the important ones later). That last thing to do before setup is complete is to create an initial post or two, just like you would on your personal page. Create an introductory post as though no one knows who you are or what you're offering, and include a relevant image or video. This initial post will be like a landing page for a short period of time.

A special note on Facebook storefronts: in 2015 Facebook began implementing a native storefront function into business pages, allowing you to sell products or services directly from your profile and negating the need to send your traffic to an external website. As of this writing the feature isn't entirely public; while it's made available to some users it's still in development and subject to constant change while they work out the kinks. While you can utilize third-party apps to serve create storefronts on Facebook, this book's focus is utilize Facebook almost exclusively. Since we can't speak to how trustworthy any third-party app is, and we can't guarantee that Facebook's storefront feature will be available to you specifically, moving forward we'll simply pretend those options don't exist and instead will focus on making a profit by directing user traffic to your external websites that are already processing transactions.

Chapter 1 Fundamental Concepts & Resources for Digital Marketing

In this chapter I aim to cover the fundamental concepts of digital marketing. An understanding of these principles is required to fully grasp the marketing strategies and tactics presented later in this guide. A number of useful resources to help you enter the world of digital marketing are also provided, for instance how you can get a unique company logo design for as little as $5.

Target Audience

In the world of digital marketing, a solid understanding of the target audience is indeed required for success. Your target audience is the demographic of people most likely to be interested in your profile, this includes where they live, their age range, their gender distribution, and their daily habits. Understanding these key characterises is necessary to tailor your content to their interests/needs/habits, thus maximizing engagement and growth.

Value Proposition

These are the characteristics, features and aspects that make a page or product attractive to an audience. You should strive to answer the question *"why would my target audience follow this page?"* Although the followers may be unaware of a profile's value proposition, the admin must have a complete appreciation of it if he wants to reach success. If the page admin wishes to widen his target audience, he must broaden the value proposition to match the demands of new users.

What exactly does a value proposition consist of? The page below has *1.8 Million* Likes, let's try to analyse its value proposition:

Case Study Analysis: simple value proposition of "Grumpy Cat Memes"

1. Users value this page because it makes them laugh
2. Users value this page because it contains cute cats with unrealistic expressions
3. Users value this page because it conveys unlikely and relatable messages through the personification of a cat

Post Reach

The reach of a post represents the amount of people that have seen the post. These users did not necessarily interact with the post by commenting or liking it, merely how many users the post reached. This metric is very useful when calculating conversion rates – what fraction of users who viewed this post proceeded to like my page?

Importance of user engagement

Remember the profitability of any social media page is determined by user engagement. Engagement is what shows its true following and user commitment to the page. Similarly the value of many tech companies is determined by daily active users or monthly active users, not registered users. Engagement is widely recognized as a universal metric for brand value, than simple page likes. For this reason, the number of likes, on average, can be better representative of value than the amount of followers a page has.

High engagement users

These users are the key to increasing user engagement, profitability and the following of your page. High engagement users are characterised for being very extremely active on Facebook: they like many posts, they tag their friends, they send links and they post lots of comments. Acquiring this key portion of your target audience is what will give your Facebook page immense visibility, engagement and a rapid growth.

Useful Resources

Bitly.com – Track how many times a URL is clicked over time. This resource is free and very easy to understand.

Fiverr.com – Here you can get a wide amount of jobs done for just $5. I recommend using it for one-off tasks. Typical things it can be used for: design brand logos, graphic design, writing item descriptions, writing biographies, etc…

Upwork.com – This website is perfect to hire Freelancers for extended work projects. You can advertise job posts, applications and –for important jobs – I recommend arranging Skype interviews. You can hire anyone from Indian customer service employee in India to an MBA graduate working for 120$/hr

Wix.com – Free resource to create & publish your own website. For simple websites, it is easy and quick to use.

Wordpress.com – Free to create a website, but you must pay for hosting fees and domain. This framework is used to build large and complicated sites, but takes time to learn how to do so efficiently.

Pixabay.com – This is my favourite website for copyright-free images. It is important to use images without copyright in all of your entrepreneurial activities!

Chapter 2 The Importance of a Facebook Page

Small and medium-sized businesses (SMEs) can use Facebook marketing strategies with high margins of success. In fact, with more than 2 billion active users every month, it is impossible to remove the blue social from your web marketing plan.

What Could Be the Goals of Facebook Marketing Referring to SMEs?

1. Brand Awareness

Facebook is a very important tool that enables SMEs to make their products and services known, while at the same time cultivating a very direct relationship with interested users.

If on the one hand, your community that is made up of people who already know your products, can follow us on the blue social, then, on the other side, it is possible to reach people who do not know us through spontaneous sharing or through sponsored ones. The latter, through the creation of the right audience, allows reaching to new people potentially interested in our products.

2. Customer Care

Facebook is also one of the websites that best lend themselves to customer care, which is assistance to its customers. Indeed, given the announcement of future updates of the algorithm of the views of the News Feed, focus on customer care could also prove successful in terms of awarding the content posted.

Promotional content can still be valid, but using your own social page as a place to solve problems and perplexities of its users can be a key to use highly because it can trigger conversations between friends, debates, and an engagement appreciated by Facebook algorithms.

3. Direct Sales

Facebook can also be used to sell your products or services. Like an e-commerce site, the platform lends itself to the possibility of direct purchase from the page, with huge benefits for users. For SMEs, this opportunity is an important resource for saving resources that would otherwise have to be spent on the creation and management of an entire site.

Obviously, it must be said that those who hold an important business cannot simply rely on the social network of Zuckerberg to market their products online, but it is a fact that not a month passes in which the Menlo Park team does not make availability of some new function that favors those who want to sell via the web.

How to Create a Facebook Marketing Strategy That Works?

Before starting to take action on Facebook, it is good for SMEs to devote time to creating a well-designed communication plan.

First of all, the goals of the strategies to be put in place must be defined.

As for the content, it will be good to dedicate only 20% of them to the promotion of your products or services, so as not to tire the user with continuous offers and hype.

Finally, the tools for checking the results must not be forgotten, with the choice of the most appropriate metrics to follow in order to understand the effectiveness of the steps taken along the road to achieving the designated objectives. For example, if the setting up of a valid customer care campaign has been done, one of the ways to evaluate the effectiveness of the actions carried out is the analysis of the number and quality of comments received, rather than that of 'likes'.

Chapter 3 Choosing Your Audience

Now that you are familiar with the basics of using Facebook ads, it's time to talk about the Facebook's ad targeting technology. This feature makes Facebook ads unique from other advertising platforms. Google Ads uses search queries and the person's search history for targeting their ads. However, aside from these information, the search giant actually has a limited information about the users interacting with their ad network. This is the reason why we often see mismatched ads when using Google.

Facebook ads aim to fix this. Facebook has a lot of raw information about their users. Just by signing up, they will know your age, name, location and email address. Most companies would go to great lengths to get these information from their target market. Facebook, however, takes it a bit further. The moment you start adding friends, Facebook's AI algorithm is able to associate certain characteristics with your account. The more you interact with the system, the more information the ad algorithm has on you. This lets the ad targeting technology know what types of ads will likely work for you.

Every user on Facebook is profiled in a similar way. The social network giant keeps track of all the things you like and don't like. They keep track of the posts that made you unfollow certain people and pages.

This is great news for marketers. Because of Facebook's meticulous data gathering, we can be rest assured that our ads will be shown to the correct people. It's just a matter of getting your targeting setting right. Let's begin with learning about the targeting options available for Facebook ads:

Here are some of the audience demographic information that you should focus on first:

- *Age group*

The age group and your market's location are the two most important information that you need to consider. You want to keep your targeting to just the right amount of audience to make sure that you are not wasting money on unwanted views. By limiting your ads to show only to a specific age group, you make sure that only people who are interested in your product will see your ad. This is particularly important if you are selling a product or service that is more likely to be bought by young and middle-aged adults.

If this is the case, you do not want your ads to show up in the screens of people who are too young. These people may not be interested in the product or service you are offering. These views will only be wasted when shown to lower age groups.

By controlling the age range of your ad targeting, you are also making sure that your ad is only shown to people who have the money to buy your product or service. While Facebook users can range from 13 and up, you must filter your views to users who are older than 18 years old. Most users who are in the 18 to 22 age range do not have a lot of disposable income yet, especially for luxurious items. If your product is on the expensive side, you may want to make sure that you target only the people who are capable of paying for it.

The best age range to target fall in the 25-32 age range. People in this age range are more likely to be employed with no parental commitments yet. They are more open to spending on less important things. People aged between 30 and 40 are likely to be starting out a family. If your product or service is related to this life milestone, you may want to limit your ad targeting to this age group. This includes products such as homeware, small homes, second hand cars and family related insurance.

- Location

Next to the age range, you also need to specify the location where the ad will be shown. For most people, picking a place to publish ads to is easy. They just need to specify the serviceable area of their business. Facebook allows you to target people in a certain location. You can then use Google Maps to specify the location where your ads will show.

There are multiple ways for you to indicate the geographical location where you want to show your ads. The easiest way is to indicate the name of the city, town, state or country in the location field. You just need to type the name of the location and select the correct one from the suggestions of places that drops down. You may also add multiple different locations to the list so your ads would show in more than one place on the map.

If you choose to use this method, the ads will be shown to users within the border of the location you indicated. This method is effective when you are targeting users from a specific town, city or even an entire country. The geographical boundaries of these locations become the limits of the location where your ads will be shown.

Another way to pinpoint the location is by dropping a location pin on the map. You can zoom in and out of the map to place the pin accurately. After placing the location pin on the map, you then have the option to choose the radius of the circle that you want for your ad targeting. If you choose 10 miles for example, your ad will be shown in a 10 mile location from the location of the pin.

This method is better suited if you are targeting people in the vicinity of a specific place. If you have a store for example, you could put the pin on the location of your store on the map. You could then assign a targeting radius of 3 miles. Your ads will be shown to Facebook users within a 3-mile radius from your store. This kind of targeting makes more sense for small businesses because they are able to target the people near them. These people are more likely to become customers.

You can show your ad to any location on the globe where there are Facebook users. If you are managing the advertising for an international brand, you can use Facebook ads to attract users to a website or an app. You can use the ads to attract users that your marketing would not be able to reach otherwise with the use of traditional advertising.

This is particularly useful if you are selling digital products or services. You will be able to show your digital wares to people who may have shown interest to similar products in the past. Even if your company is based in the US for example, you will be able to show your products to people in other countries where Facebook is also popular.

Facebook uses multiple location indicators to pinpoint the location of users. For mobile users, they may use the GPS on their phone to find out where the person is located. Desktop users on the other hand may be located using the location feature on the computer they are using. If they fall within the location that you indicated in your ad targeting, your ad can end up getting promoted their accounts.

- *Men vs Women*

You may also want to specify whether you want your ads shown solely to men or women. Ideally, you need to create a separate ad campaign for men and for women. Each sex has different interests and motivations for buying. They are also attracted to different ad creatives. Ad creatives refer to the visual aspect of the ad. It may include images and texts and the other visual elements that can be manipulated in the ad.

Even when advertising the same product to men and women, you will need to use a different ad campaign for each sex. Men are attracted to different colors and ad copies when compared to women. By targeting both sexes with the same set of ads, you are compromising between the two and this may make your ads less effective in attracting and converting people.

Detailed Targeting

While the age group and location of your audience will narrow down your ad target, it will still be too broad if you do not include other demographical information. Facebook allows you to target your audience even more accurately by allowing more filters in the Detailed Targeting section of the ad creation process. This section includes fields where you can add additional demographical information as well as target audience interest and behaviors.

To further boost the accuracy of your ads, you could type a characteristic of your target audience in the field provided. For instance, you may write the brand of a product that you are competing with. By targeting this specific brand, you will be able to show your ads to customers and the fans of your competitors.

If you are targeting mobile users only, you may specify the brand of phone that they are using. If you write the word iPhone in the field for example, you will find different options for targeting. They are usually labelled as "Interests", "Demographics" or "Behavior." They may also be labelled as a type of demographical information like "School", "Employer" or "Field of Study."

You could also choose to target people who own an iPhone 6, 7 or any other common types of iPhone. You may also target people who are generally interested in the iPhone as a subject. Interest means that they may have liked iPhone related content in the past. This could also mean that they reacted positively to pages, posts and comments related to iPhones. Your Detailed Targeting field will look like this:

INCLUDE people who match at least ONE of the following
Behaviors > Mobile Device User > All Mobile Devices by Brand > Apple

> OWNS: IPHONE 7
>
> OWNS: IPHONE 6

Following this example, your ad will be shown to Facebook users who own either an iPhone 7 or iPhone 6. This means that your ad will be shown to two groups of people. You could add more groups of people by adding more interest, behavior or demographical information in this field. The more you add to this list, the broader your target audience becomes.

The targeting information you include in these fields will be used together with the age group, sex and location information you entered previously to make further narrow down the audience of your ad. In Facebook Ad Manager, you will see an audience meter in the side of the screen that will indicate how narrow your targeting is. The meter will indicate if your *audience is too narrow, just right or too broad*. The information around the audience meter will also indicate how many people in your chosen location falls within your target audience.

If there are too few people to target (Narrow), the Facebook ads algorithm may not be able to deliver your ads. Your ad may just expire without getting a single impression or click. If the targeting is too broad on the other hand, your ads will be shown even to people who may not be interested in your product or service.

Use the audience meter to adjust your targeting information for your ad. A healthy target audience will make the audience meter pointer point on the green portion of the meter (Just Right).

If your targeting is too narrow, you can broaden it by adding more interests, behaviors or demographical information. You may also widen the age range and the location targeting of your ads.

If the targeting is too broad, however, you can also do the opposite. You could remove some of the interest, behavior and demographical targeting, as well as lessen the age range and the location radius.

Targeting a Subset of your Broad Audience (Narrowing Further)

You also have an option to target a part of a broader audience to further narrow your ads' audience. You can do this through the "Narrow Further" link in the bottom of the Detailed Targeting section of the ad editor. By using this feature, you will be able to target audiences using two or more interests. Let's say that you want to target iPhone users who are also Los Angeles Lakers fans. You could indicate the Los Angeles Lakers as an interest in the "INCLUDE people who match at least ONE of the following" field. You could then use the "Narrow Further" link to show the "and MUST ALSO match at least ONE of the following" field. You could use this field to target users who are using iPhone 6 and 7. In the end, your targeting fields will look something like this:

INCLUDE people who match at least ONE of the following
Interests > Additional Interests

LOS ANGELES LAKERS

and MUST ALSO match at least ONE of the following

Behaviors > Mobile Device User > All Mobile Devices by Brand > Apple

> OWNS: IPHONE 7
>
> OWNS: IPHONE 6

By using this kind of arrangement, you are targeting people who are interested in the Los Angeles Lakers (NBA team) and also owns an iPhone 7, an iPhone 6 or both phones. Your ad will not show to just any user who has shown interest towards the Los Angeles Lakers. They must also own the iPhones indicated in the targeting fields for the ads to show in their account.

With this feature, you are able to gain even more control over the people who see you ad. However, you also run the danger of making your targeting too narrow.

Excluding Groups of People

In the same line where you'll find the "Narrow Further" link, you will also see the "Exclude People" link. This way, you can choose to exclude people who have specific interests and behaviors. You can also pick more than one characteristic to identify the people that you want to exclude.

Budget and Duration

After setting the target information for your ads, the next step is to set your budget and the running duration for your Facebook ad campaign. The right budget will vary depending on the location where you want to show your ads and the general competition level in that location. You will also need a bigger budget if you are advertising in a location where many other people and businesses are advertising. If you are the only person advertising in a particular place on the other hand, you can get by with a budget as low as $5 per day.

Aside from the competition from other advertisers, your budget will also be affected by the goal of your advertising campaign. If you only want to get post impressions or page likes, $5 per day is enough to get a decent amount of views in a location with low competition. If you want to drive traffic to a website on the other hand, you will need to assess the cost per click on your ad to know the exact amount that you will need to get a decent amount of views. Luckily, you will be able to adjust your demographical information to try to decrease the cost per click of your campaign. To achieve this however, there will be plenty of trial and error.

Facebook makes the financial side of your campaign transparent even before you start it. When setting a budget for instance, the Facebook ad editor will tell you how much money you will need for your ad to run for the duration you specify. You can adjust your daily ad budget and the duration to have control over the overall spending of the campaign.

You also have the option to run the ad campaign continuously. You just need to set a daily budget for the ad and it will continue to run until you manually stop it. Be careful with this setting though because this will lead to a monthly deduction from your credit card. If you forget that you have a Facebook ad running, you may be surprised by the ad campaign amounts on your credit card bill.

After setting up the ad budget and duration, the next step is to add a payment option for your ad campaign. The available payment options vary per country. The most commonly used mode of payment are credit cards and debit cards. If you choose to use a card, Facebook will do a test transaction on it to make sure that it is still active. If the transaction is successful, you will be able to start your promotion. Otherwise, you will need to add another mode of payment that Facebook can verify.

Refining your ad targeting

You cannot expect to get your desired results after just one Facebook ad campaign. By researching in advance, you may be able to experience some level of success. However, you will always find points where you can further improve your ad's performance. You can do this by adjusting the targeting mechanism of your ads.

An example of this is by targeting different age groups with your ads. You can create three different ad campaigns where the difference is the age group. One campaign may target 21-25 year-olds with the second and third campaigns targeting the 26-30 and 31-35 age groups respectively. If all other characteristics aside from the age group are similar, you will be able to compare the effectiveness of your ad according to the age group.

The general goal when refining your targeting data is to minimize the cost of advertising. Targeting issues will lead to a low conversion rate. In Facebook, conversion rate is calculated by the number of conversions (desired outcome) divided by the impressions (the number of times an ad is shown). The result is then multiplied by 100% to convert it to percent. The lower your conversion rate, the more expensive the ad campaign becomes. Most of the time, a low conversion rate is a result of poor targeting.

You can further improve the performance and efficiency of the ad by experimenting on different changes on the targeting of the ads. Your goal is to find a group of people that you can convert but aren't targeted by other marketers in your niche market.

Chapter 4 Choose & refine your page theme

Any successful Facebook page must be centred on a single, well-defined theme. Whether fitness, flowers, cars, a brand or a person's life— your page must contain content only relating to this theme. Write down your page theme using pen and paper in a couple of words maximum, read it and see if it matches your vision for the page. By writing it down, the page theme becomes a final target set within your mind. When choosing a page theme you should follow these two criteria if your goal is to build a large following.

Criteria #1— you must be knowledgeable and passionate about this theme. During the early stages of your page you will have to do extensive amounts of market analysis, assessing the competitors and search for *that little something* that makes your page unique. You will have to dedicate a lot of time and effort to this task, if it covers something you love it will be far simpler and more enjoyable.

Criteria #2—the theme must appeal to a large number of people if you want to reach a millions of users. You might have a very strong passion for Japanese ants, but I am afraid you might be one of very few people interested in the subject… *your target audience is simply too small.* A page can engage millions of users only if millions of people are interested in its message (value proposition). A great suggestion is to start on a broader theme, test out different markets and direct your page where you encounter the most positive user feedback.

After you have refined your theme to a sufficiently small target audience and your value proposition perfectly matches the market needs, you will acquire very loyal and highly engaged users following your Facebook page. *These users will drive the growth of your page.* Once you have acquired all/most of users in this niche you can broaden your content and value proposition to incorporate a wider audience. This is how you build market domination over social media.

Example strategy

An example of an initial broad theme is *luxury travel*. After evaluating initial feedback, you may choose to test out narrower themes of private jet chartering, white-sand Caribbean beaches and yacht sailing. After detailed feedback evaluation, you might see yacht sailing receives highest user engagement, so that is what you focus your page on (you might want to refine your theme page further i.e. catamaran/race boats…, but for the sake of this example it is not necessary). Now, that your page is highly focused to a specific niche, you can produce content that perfectly meets the wishes of yacht sailing-enthusiasts. You will build and acquire very high-engagement users who love your content and have a high page-loyalty. After capturing the majority of the audience in your niche (i.e. your page is no longer growing) you can expand the breadth of your page to expand your target audience and hence acquire new customers. You will maintain most of the high-engagement followers acquired due their emotional investment in your page, but you are now able to approach an entirely new target audience. As you begin to dominate more and more niches, you decide to broaden your page again to target much wider markets and audiences.

This is the key to building a massive following: refine your page to a specific niche (refined theme) until you dominate that market, then target another niche and dominate it, so forth.

Chapter 5 Using advertising functions on Facebook

Facebook has options to pay for advertising in addition to utilizing the offers page on their site. Paying for advertising that will post to people outside of your current following will ensure that you are reaching potential followers and clients that you are not already reaching. This is perhaps the most recognizable method as compared to traditional marketing. Essentially, you are paying to run a print ad on Facebook.

To get this done, click the "Promote" button on the sidebar of your Facebook page. A pop-up will surface giving you the options. The first option allows you to pay to get more clicks for a fixed monthly fee. This feature allows you to post several ads throughout the month for one rate. Get started by creating an ad and choosing what demographics you would like to reach. Facebook does the rest. While the benefits can be clear, be sure to use material that is targeted to your specific demographic audience. This feature also allows you to choose a region in which to send out the random ads. This is important if the majority of your business is run at a specific geographical location. Sending out ads to people over one hundred miles away is a bit of a waste, but targeting people within a twenty or fifty-mile radius is more likely to land you more customers. Of course, you also want these people to follow your page to increase your organic reach, so make sure your ad has some sort of offer for liking the page.

Any time you promote a post, you have the option to expand your audience. Honestly, why would you not choose this option? You can advertise to more people for the same price. When setting up your ad, under audience choose the box that says "People who like your page AND their friends" to ensure the broadest reach.

The promote feature also allows you to set up a promotion specifically for your page. This is where a crafty description of your page comes in handy. In case you're not good at creating media on your own, Facebook automatically generates an ad that can be used to get started. It usually contains your cover art and the description of your page. Like the other promotion, it can be sent to specific demographics, and the rates are based per click. Simply pick a daily budget to stick to, like five to ten dollars. On average, one dollar gets you two clicks, but will, of course, depend on the quality of content you put out there. Do the math backward to determine your budget. If your goal is to get 100 new likes this month, that will require about $50, or about $2 per day. While the results are not guaranteed, they do have a good track record.

A newer feature in Facebook's advertising lineup it the addition of the paid sign up. This feature allows ads to go out that promote your page and encourage people to sign up. Similar to the page promotion feature, this pay per click option adds a button that signs people up to follow your site directly. That is, it takes one click instead of a few. Remember that followers can be lazy on social media and the simpler you make things for them, the better the response. Again, the feature allows you to pick a demographic region to advertise to and offers the ability to post across to Instagram, increasing your reach.

An old feature, but a great feature is the 'boost post. This gives you the ability to utilize the data you gathered from your page insights. If you had a post that did exceptionally better than the rest, choose to boost and advertise this post. For example, if you own a clothing store and people went wild for a new brand of jeans you are carrying, the business would likely benefit from rerunning this ad to a new set of people. Yes, creating a similar post with the same information to your regulars will certainly keep the excitement going, but bringing this viral sensation to others in your region who have not seen it yet will boost business and increase your page following. This feature is all about finding untapped potential customers and getting your message out there. The benefit here is that you already know your post was well received, so boosting it for a small fee can ensure that the strangers in your target audience will like it too.

The only problem with boosted posts is that they appear as a "Suggested Post" on a person's newsfeed. This is code for "paid advertisement," and the tendency to scroll right past is increased. While this may ultimately leave you with less exposure than intended, it is still much better than putting nothing at all out there. Any exposure, even if it doesn't immediately lead to increased clicks or following will bring brand awareness to your business. While the payoff isn't always swift, people will remember it. Paired with marketing in other mediums can help create the brand awareness required to become a household name.

Yes, this feature works, but it should be met with some hesitation. That is, test the ad in a small market before you spend a large amount of money trying to reach millions. The marketing budget will take a huge hit if you invest in an ad on a product that has lost its luster. Any old-school marketer will tell you this works, regardless of internet ads or traditional television or print advertising. Pick a small demographic, and invest a maximum of $50 per month. Give it thirty days and keep an eye on the paid reach on your insights page and compare it to organic reach. If your paid reach increases your organic reach exponentially, you will know that the ad you chose was a good investment, and still provides relevant content to your audience. If not, experiment with a few different kinds of posts to really understand why boosting did not work.

If your ad was an overnight success and you insist on upping your budget, keep an eye on those stats. All content gets old and overplayed.

Begin to recognize when interest begins to trend down and reinvent your advertising idea. The worst mistake to make is assuming that a good marketing plan will always be good. We must adapt and change to the sales climate. Staying the same means your business will get stagnant. A good way to recognize this is with your likes and following. As likes begin to trickle off or followers disappear, that is a good indication that you need to reinvent your campaign. Waiting too long to do this will make your page and brand less relevant.

Remember that business trends on social media often follow trends that you have recognized in sales. Learn to work with these ebbs and flows to drive more business during slow times, and sell more when you already have the attention of your customers. This is especially true with seasonal businesses. Take the landscaping business discussed earlier. This company can promote services in the snow season while things begin to wind down with lawn care. In addition to hooking more snow accounts, they can sell the same customers on a salt and sand package while the customer is already engaged and thinking about their needs. This is the best time to strike, driving sales and boosting online presence.

It may not be appropriate to boost posts or locally promote all the time, if at all. If your organic reach is already growing your business exponentially, don't bother boosting posts. If you feel your following growth has slowed, try boosting a post to jumpstart traffic again. Just watch your insights instead of blindly spending your marketing budget. Know your market and best times to promote, just as you would for in-store ads and newspaper marketing.

Chapter 6 How to Grow Your Business with Facebook Advertising

Social network websites take up more than 20% of all online advertisements. This information tells us just how much social media advertising has grown in popularity over the years. Businesses worldwide are recognizing the potential that social media has to grow their business. Social media advertising helps you grow your business in numerous ways such as:

- delivering your advertisements directly in front of the targeted audience;
- enabling tracking and reviewing the consumer's behaviors on all stages of their journey from engagement to conversion;
- consistent insights into the online activities and behaviors of your consumer base that are relevant to your business and brand; and
- consistent media to reach and communicate with your consumers

The nature of social media networks like Facebook allows businesses to gain fast and efficient information on consumer needs and preferences, which are otherwise the data they would only be able to acquire through costly research and extensive surveys.

But not everyone is equally effective with Facebook advertising. Many businesses fail to create effective marketing campaigns, which results in major budget losses. For starters, you must understand that the main requirements for effective social network advertising are:

- advertisement content and website links that are relevant and beneficial to the targeted audience, and
- valuable pieces of information that you can easily incorporate into your current marketing strategy.

Advertising on Facebook is done through the network's on-site application, the Ads Manager, which all users can use to design their own advertising campaigns and post the advertisements to the website.

Once you create your Facebook ads, you can then target your ideal audience by location, gender, age, online activities and behaviors, relationship status, job title, college or workplace. Once you select your target audience, Facebook will show you the exact number of potential ad viewers.

Why Are Facebook Ads Helpful in Growing Your Business?

Facebook ads carry the potential for business growth because the users interact with the advertisement the same way they interact with other Facebook users. They can "Like" or "Share" the ad, and they can also participate in the discussion in the comment section. When the viewers of your ad are actively discussing its content, your advertisement will appear on the pages of their "Friends", further spreading the word about your business and your message.

Facebook's Ads Manager provides you with extensive reports on how your ads are performing. These reports also contain information on the click-through rate, or the number of clicks that the ads have received, as well as the breakdown of the viewer's activities and the activities of their contacts related to the advertisement. The network will deliver reports that speak about the efficiency of your campaign, which allows you to track progress. One of the most telling pieces of information is the number of clicks that is calculated based on the amount of time the users have clicked the ad and landed on the advertising page, Liked a page, or RSVP'd to an event that you've been advertising.

How Are You Paying for Facebook Advertising?

There are a couple of ways in which the network charges you for the ad placement. CPC, or cost-per-click, is a unit that measures the charge of a single click or interaction with your ad. CPC also includes Likes, Shares, and Comments, covering all of the activities of your audience on the paid post. You can choose whether or not to set a budget for the ad. If you set a fixed budget, your card will be charged the maximum set amount, and the network will run your campaign until the cost reaches the maximum budget amount. If you don't limit your advertising budget, the network will run your campaign until the funds on your credit or debit card are exhausted.

Aside from setting the overall campaign budget, you can also set a daily budget for your campaign. The daily budget is the limit you will spend on each individual ad and ad set each day. If you set a daily budget limit, the network will run your ads until it reaches the set amount.

What Is a Facebook Marketing Campaign?

A Facebook marketing campaign is a group of ads that you create based on your overall marketing strategy and advertising goals. When designed and planned strategically, Facebook ads will benefit your business because they allow you to group them and segment the audience, sending your message to the most receptive viewer group.

Every Facebook user can create their own advertising campaign. To create a Facebook advertising campaign, you have to have a Facebook profile. You have to have your own profile page, and you can create your advertisement by clicking the "Add Advert" link. There you will fill out a page and complete the details of the advert that you are trying to make. The design of the ad also includes a link to the target destination. The ad needs to contain a title, a body, and the text that describes the ad. You need to choose an image that will be appropriate for the ad, like a business logo, an image of the product, or another image of your choice.

Ad Targeting

Facebook focuses its strategy on the enormous number of its members and leverages this number to offer advertisers the possibility of focused targeting from a broad demographic. Unlike other advertising platforms, the Facebook Ads Manager carries an advantage in terms of giving you the opportunity to select the audience that will view your ad. This way, you have the ability to not only design the ad to cater to your target audience but to also control who will view your ad, meaning that your budget will be spent only on viewers you find desirable for your campaign.

Facebook allows targeting based on demographic profiles and interests that users reveal on their pages. The chances of having a cost-friendly campaign increase with a variety of targeting options. Well-optimized targeting can make a true difference in terms of driving traffic to your website. Sophisticated targeting is all about making sure that your target consumer gives attention to your advertisement. While there's a limit to the amount of data you can collect about prospective consumers, leveraging the available ones in the smartest way is still an option many businesses use to their greatest advantage. Your goal is for your campaign to target those consumers who are most likely to interact with it.

Click-through rates increase when the advertisements are customized by criteria like location, content visited, or the information searched on search engines. While consumers like relevance, they are easily annoyed. If the ads are tailored to their interests and are relevant, consumers are more likely to interact. The effectiveness of the ad depends on the type of profile information that is being used. Demographics, gender preferences, location, and interests have the most important role.

After defining the goal of your marketing campaign, your next step is to define your target audience. The Facebook Ads Manager allows you to choose the viewers of your ad by parameters such as the location, demographics, age, gender, likes, and interests.

Aside from basic targeting, you can also use the advance demographic settings, which include birthday, relationship status, gender interest, languages, education, and work.

How to Manage the Advertising Budget

Facebook gives you plenty of tools to plan and manage your advertising budget.

Setting Up Pricing and Schedule

To run your advertising campaign, you will need to complete the account currency, the time zone, the campaign budget, the ad schedule, and the pricing. Upon completing these steps, you can review your campaign and make any additional desired changes before placing an advertisement order. Having full control of your spending is another benefit to advertising with Facebook. For example, if you paid for a TV or newspaper ad placement, you would have no control over the delivery and efficiency of your ads. On the other hand, Facebook allows you to go back, review your campaign, and make all the necessary adjustments to both keep your ads and audience effective while also controlling your costs.

Create a Community of Supporters

As a business, you can create group pages where your followers don't have to accept you as a "Friend". Instead, the user can simply click "Become a fan" or "Like". Once you publish a Facebook post, it will appear on all of the members' pages. The fan will continue to receive updates from your page unless they "Unlike" your page.

Free Visibility and Referrals

Another advantage of this method of advertising is that your fans' interactions with the page are also visible on their friends' pages. Every time your fan makes an interaction with the page, it will appear on their friend's homepage. This way, you can share both your company information as well as photos, videos, applications, comments, and messages for free.

An Identity Behind the Brand

A Facebook page reveals the identity behind your business to potential customers. This way, your consumer base gets to view you as a personable, human entity instead of an anonymous business that's presented with the other advertising formats. When you build up your business page and form a consistent relationship with the audience, your consumers know what they can expect from your business. This will help them build up trust and secure a friendly relationship with your business.

Why Do You Need a Marketing Strategy?

A marketing strategy is vital for Facebook advertising. A marketing strategy defines:

- what are you trying to achieve with your campaign;

- how to get there; and

- which consumers to target.

To start with, it is essential for you to define a campaign goal. You will base your entire marketing strategy on this goal. Your entire campaign concept needs to revolve around the target audience and their features, particularly when creating the ad description, content, and visuals.

Challenges of Advertising on Facebook

Saturation

While social media advertising remains the most budget-friendly and the best-optimized form of advertising, the saturation of the platform poses a challenge. Your potential user can interact with as many businesses as they want, as well as their contacts. Since it's impossible for Facebook to provide the same level of exposure for everyone, there are different priorities (and algorithms) being applied to secure prioritizing according to the user's interest.

Competition, Recognition, and Relevance

Due to the saturation of the platform, as well as the immense amount of competition, becoming recognized is a challenge. More than that, staying relevant on the platform will require continuous work considering the billions of posts that are being published every single day. Becoming recognized and staying relevant on the platform will require the application of an intelligent strategy.

Create a Community and Increase Engagement

Create a Community Page

When Facebook first launched their community page, they wanted to focus on nonbusiness topics. Facebook CEO Mark Zuckerberg and his team felt they needed to differentiate official business pages from nonbusiness pages, such as fan pages. Unfortunately, this created a lot of confusion and misunderstanding with community pages. An example of a community page is cooking, cleaning, and gardening. The information on community pages is easily found on the internet. However, Facebook users who share an interest in cooking or gardening can connect with each other through the community page.

Over the last few years, a lot has changed with community pages. First, they have become more business friendly. At first, many businesses were frustrated with their community pages because they had no control over them. While people can still create a community page for your business, you are also able to create your own. You can do this as you set up your official business page.

There are three main reasons you want to investigate creating a community page for your business. First, you will have control over the page. Second, community pages are less official than an official business page. This gives you another avenue to understand your audience, which can help you with your marketing strategy. Third, people will share information that they aren't comfortable sharing on an official page.

To create a community page:

1. Go to https://www.facebook.com/pages/creation/ and click the "get started" button under the "Community of Public Figure" option.

2. Enter the type of community and page name.

3. Upload a profile picture and cover photo. If you are creating a community page for your business, you can upload pictures of your building, logo, or a group photograph of your employees.

4. Write your business information in the "About" section. Make sure you take time to edit the information.

5. Ensure that all your information is on the community page, such as business hours, location, contact, and any other information.

6. Share your page with your Facebook friends.

Increase Engagement

One way to know people are noticing your business is through Facebook. When you set up an official business page, you will receive statistical information. For example, you will learn how many people like your page on a weekly basis, like your posts, saw your posts, and clicked any links. To help you notice your business's progress, it's a good idea to keep track of this information. You can do this through Facebook or by recording the information.

Like most people, you will be glued to the amount of attention your posts receive, especially when you are starting. Don't become discouraged if you feel people aren't paying attention to your page. It takes time to build a business and increase engagement. Instead of slowly watching the numbers increase, incorporate some of these tips to help boost engagement.

1. Create posts where people need to answer a question. Don't make it a complicated question. Ask them something that pertains to your business. For example, if you have a flower shop, you can ask them "What is your favorite flower?" You can also ask them a question where they have to fill in the blank. For instance, "A ____ flower follows the sun." You could allow them to guess for fun or have a contest where the first correct response receives a prize.

2. Give an inside look into your company. You can do this by taking photographs of your lobby, office, or your employees.

3. If you notice one of your fans shared something relevant to your business, share it on your page. This can make someone feel special and also help start a conversation.

4. Give your fans a reason to smile. Do something special for the people who are following your page. This could be anything from a quote that's relevant to your business to having a customer appreciation day. You also don't need to be serious all the time. If you come across a joke that's relevant, post it. Laughing is a way to keep people engaged.

5. Pay attention to what posts are liked more. You might notice a trend with the time frame or what type of content you are posting.

6. Use images as much as possible. People often stop scrolling to look at images and are more likely to engage.

Become Personable & Accessible

Customer service is one of the most important characteristics of a company. Whether you are conversing with a customer face-to-face, over the phone, or online you want to be personable. This can often be overlooked through Facebook because you don't have to worry about your facial expressions, voice tone, and body language. You do need to pay attention to the words and phrases you use, your punctuation, spelling, and written tone.

No matter how you converse, you always need to be respectful. This is often easy to do when people leave good reviews or comments. Unfortunately, not every review or comment you receive will be positive. It's easy to respond negatively after reading a rude comment. You want to do what you can to respond politely and respectfully even when a customer does not. Think of it this way – everyone who visits that post can read the comments. They will read the upset customer's comment and yours. How you respond is going to reflect on your business.

Accessibility is another way to be personable and gain followers. People use Facebook for a variety of reasons. For example, they might be searching for the nearest flower shop when they come across your page. They would like to order a certain flower but aren't sure if you have it in stock, so they send you a direct message. Responding to that message as soon as possible is going to benefit your company. In fact, it could help you make a sale.

Learn Customer Needs & Preferences

You need to get to know your customers so you can learn how your business can benefit them. When people are going to pay to use a service, they want to make sure there is something that will help them. For example, you are promoting your new product on your Facebook page, but it's not generating engagements. You look at the post and notice it simply describes the product. There is nothing that helps connect the product to your customer. You then create a new Facebook post about the product that focuses on how it will benefit the customer. This post is going to generate more interest because you have focused on your customer's needs.

Optimize your Landing Page

If you're designing an ad that links to your website, be it a blog or a shopping page, optimizing that page to align with the campaign has a major role in generating conversions. One of the ways to make your Facebook advertising campaign more effective is to align your landing page with your ad in terms of style, tone, content, and esthetics.

Keyword Research and Context

While keyword research is a useful part of the targeting, it is not the method that speaks the most about customer needs and preferences. While keyword research may reveal the topics that the users are most interested in, it can't reveal the intention and circumstances surrounding these searches. Keyword research, while useful, lacks context. To uncover the issues surrounding the search interest and the intention, you can try to research the questions that the audience is asking that are relevant to your industry. There are numerous websites that focus on answering an indefinite number of questions. The great news is that all of these websites are free to use. You can use them to not only research the customer pain points but also answer the questions yourself, giving educated advice from an expert point of view.

Finding out what bothers your customers by reading the top-rated and most popular questions within your industry is a lot more informative and time effective than running keyword research and analyzing the extensive amounts of information. By reading and answering the burning questions relevant to your industry and consumers, you are both learning about the pain points and building your business's online reputation.

Aside from pain points, researching questions will give you a glimpse into the background, context, and circumstances that the user faces related to the problem, which you can leverage to craft quality content and upscale your posts using storytelling.

Research Feedback

In addition, reading the feedback that the audience gives to the relevant products and services gives you insight into their needs and wants. Consumers leave very honest, blunt, and unbiased feedback. Reading this feedback could tell you about the details that customers care about, but otherwise aren't mentioning. Such details might include shipping and delivery, pet peeves related to the size and shape of the product, as well as minor to major troubles the consumers have when using the product.

Expert Search Engine Optimization (SEO) Tools

While traditional SEO techniques are effective in helping you pinpoint the right audience members, there are a number of other tools that can help you as well. Using keyword analysis software, you can trace the keywords and key phrases that the consumers are searching. You can use these keywords to optimize your content in a way that highlights the exact problems that the customers are researching. SEO tools are particularly effective with PPC campaigns. They can help you identify the right ideas for your content, whether it's a particular ad, your landing page, or the content of your landing page.

Stalk the Competition

By analyzing the discussions on your competitors' pages, you can also track the typical problems that users are having with their products and services, as well as the problems that are driving them to seek the product as a solution.

Chapter 7 Making Ads - Targeting

Targeting is absolutely the most skillful part of Facebook advertising. You can test your images and copy until you have an optimized advertisement. You cannot magically come up with the creative targeting that is truly the secret sauce of a successful Facebook campaign.

I'm not really sure what you expected to get when you opened his book. It's fairly likely that you expected to get a blueprint of how to advertise on Facebook. I simply could have delivered that model, but I would have been shortchanging you.

Advertising, in general, is a battle of wits, direct competition, and psychology. None of those elements are unique to advertising on Facebook. Because I really want you to advertise successfully on Facebook, we needed to discuss our approach to advertising in general. I've been weaving in the required lessons throughout the book thus far (have you noticed them?!).

One of the main general business lessons we need to discuss in this chapter is who your customer really SHOULD be, and compare it to whom your customer currently is. I've never worked with an owner who had the level of detail of an "ideal customer" that he or she needed in order to leverage fully Facebook's targeting campaign; so, no, you aren't the one exception. Complete this exercise with me and thank me later for improving your business beyond Facebook advertising.

Finding Your Ideal Audience

"The customer is always right" and "anyone who gives me business is my customer" are two phrases that freak me out when I hear them. The year is 2014 and you perceive your time to be more valuable than it has even been in your life. A customer who takes up too much of your time is not a good customer for you. A customer who causes problems left and right is not a good customer for you.

The reason why you might accept this person as your customer is because you do not have enough of your ideal customers. If I could fill your store/website with a [virtual] line out the door of your ideal customers, I'm sure you would stop accepting those crappy ones because you would no longer need them.

Well, let's do that!

Take out a pen and paper. That's right. Take out a pen and paper. If you don't have a pen and paper with you right now, close this book and perform this exercise when you have a pen and paper. *The ideal audience exercise is probably the most important exercise you will perform in the existence of your business – take it seriously.*

Beyond writing this amazing book, I offer custom Facebook advertising services. You can't come up with mesmerizing images or mind-numbingly awesome copy that is as effective as I can. You cannot split test as efficiently as me. Further, you might just not be passionate about Facebook advertising as I am and instead want to focus on other aspects of your business. Or, you might just want to know with complete certainty that your business is running elite Facebook advertising campaigns, printing you lots of money.

I have an ideal customer. Some of you will want to work with me, and frankly, I will not want to work with some of you – I say no to people all the time.

You also have an ideal customer. If you could wave a wand and create the perfect customer, how would that person look? If you would hand pick the age, interests, financial situation, passion – metaphorically mold your customer EXACTLY the way you want him or her – what would that person be? I will perform this exercise with you to give you a better idea of your considerations *and how specific you should get with your ideal audience*:

Greg's Ideal Facebook Advertising Client

• *Age 28+/Trusts My FB Knowledge.* I need mature clients. In my experience, younger people tend to think they know everything about everything. Age is a filter I use to avoid having to deal with people who want both to hire me and teach me how to do my job. I am very skilled at what I do. I can explain literally every single decision that I make and why I make those decisions (see rational thought process below). My ideal client does not question me every single step of the way.

• *Hands off Approach.* I prefer situations where I can get down to work, create advertising campaigns, and print money for my clients. I prefer not to be on the phone constantly or answering emails every 12 hours about updates on campaigns that take longer than 12 hours to provide insight.

• *Listens to my non-Facebook suggestions and actually can implement them.* Most clients think they are hiring me exclusively to provide Facebook advertising campaigns. However, after a user clicks a FB ad, he/she is taken to a landing page that needs to convert in order to make money! Luckily, I am also an expert at landing page optimization, so I have lots of valuable insight to provide when a user is on a client's site. If the client cannot update the page, or make the necessary changes, or add in pixel tracking to their pages, that is not an ideal situation for me.

• *Has a profitable business/is not strapped for cash.* I prefer not to work with individuals who *need* a Facebook campaign instantly to become profitable or their business will shut down. Luckily, Facebook campaigns are the fastest path to a profitable advertising campaign compared to everything else (social media, offline marketing, etc.) because of the scale Facebook provides; however, that scale also means we often will want to pour money into a profitable campaign as quickly as possible. You need money in order to be able to do that.

• *U.S.-based.* As of this writing, Facebook has not unlocked certain powerful advertising filters for anyone outside the United States. My ideal client is in the United States because I can make a bigger impact. If there are 10 elements to a Facebook campaign, I can be better than my client's competitors at 10 things. If there are 20 elements to a Facebook campaign, I have the opportunity to offer an even larger competitive advantage.

• *Does not care about fancy reports.* I care about a few metrics: how much it costs to get users on a client's site, how frequently those users convert into customers, and what our ROI is. I don't [directly] care about likes, or comments, or fan-page views. I want to spend my time making the best possible advertisements for clients and creating the largest ROI for them; I don't want to spend time presenting vanity metrics.

• *Thinks logically/rationally.* Lots of people are afraid to do things because they are afraid. They think emotionally as opposed to logically and rationally. My ideal client thinks logically and rationally, which matches my thought process. When both parties have an identical thought process (it doesn't have to be an identical approach), the work flow is more smoothly.

That's my ideal client. You absolutely should note that this list is very specific and likely makes me come across as VERY picky. Remember, though, this is my IDEAL client. Do I have clients who do not meet all the criteria on this list? Of course! However, the reason why we MUST create this ideal audience is because we will be targeting them on Facebook. I know it sounds crazy, but there are 1.2 billion active users on Facebook – your ideal customer exists on Facebook and we are going to find them!

DO NOT MOVE ONTO THE NEXT SECTION UNTIL YOU PERFORM THE IDEAL AUDIENCE EXERCISE. WRITE DOWN EVERY BIT OF INFORMATION YOU CAN THINK OF (INCLUDING THINGS LIKE MUSICAL TASTE, IF THAT

REALLY MATTERS TO YOU – THIS IS YOUR "IDEAL" CUSTOMER AND YOU CAN BE AS PICKY AS YOU WANT)!

Let's Go Target Your Customer!

The best way to determine which Facebook parameters to use is for us to go hand in hand through all of them. That's right – we literally are going to walk through every filtering option for Facebook targeting. You're quite welcome!

Head into power editor and return to one of the sample advertisements we created for the sample campaign. In the provided area to edit the AD SETS, hit the " edit audience" button.

Right now, we have used the "additional interests" of *cleaning*. Hover your mouse to the right of that box and hit the x that pops up to remove that filter.

We now have a clean slate (kind of – we are still filtered for "married." but we'll fix that).

Click the More Demographics button and you'll see a few options arise:

We are going to work through each of these categories first. Hover over Relationship and you'll see two options pop up: "Interested In" and "Relationship Status." Click Interested In and you'll see the following addition to your audience:

If you are looking for a specific gender preference, here is where you would make your selection (i.e., you want to write an ad that encourages buying flowers for "the woman in your life"). One note: if you are indifferent as to what gender in which your target audience is interested, do not select "unspecified." If you choose unspecified, you only will include people who have not indicated in which gender they are interested, whereas you just want all people regardless of gender.

Now go back to More Demographics, Relationship, and Relationship Status. You can choose the relationship status of your audience here (click "browse" if your menu is not expanded). You'll notice we've already selected "married," so you can remove that filter if it is unnecessary. You can choose more than one option.

Go select the four options in More Demographics, Education. You'll see you can target specific schools, fields of study, education level, and undergrad years. As a hint, you may want to target only college graduates, or if you are targeting college students, you can choose "In School." If you wanted only to target individuals who attended Ivy League schools, you would manually select the eight schools here.

By now, you should start to get a little excited about the possibilities that these other categories provide. Keep in mind that we are creating our first profile for our IDEAL CUSTOMER. If you see other categories that you think you might be interested in exploring down the road, create a document with a list of them and where they are located.

Keep going and expand all the options from within "Work." We'll now see some new box types that do not feature a browse button (employers and job titles). While employers will be fairly easy to include manually, Job Titles will be more puzzling.

If you are targeting a specific type of person, you'll have to learn the job titles that person might have. Facebook offers Job Titles like "firefighter" and "goalkeeper," but a CEO is listed under "Chief Executive Officer," "CEO & Founder," and "President/CEO." If you are unsure of the various titles your ideal audience has, you'll want to perform a Google search!

Think about the motivation for someone to post information about his/her careers (or even in general). There has to be a certain level of pride, or the desire to share information, in order for someone to let the world know. Further, different ways of describing a position indicate traits about the individual. I own businesses but my Job Title on Facebook is not "My own boss" or "Owning my own businesses" or "Living the dream." Those three examples are more likely to be tied to someone who is new to the entrepreneurial world and proud of the journey along which they are traveling. Therefore, if I wanted to target business owners of more than a few years, I would not include those job titles.

Make sure you keep your eye on the "Potential Audience" number to the right of your filters. If you pick a filter that absolutely kills your audience down to something like fewer than 1,000 people, consider removing it. You can always add something back if you need further segmentation within your audience.

You are officially familiar with all the types of boxes you'll encounter. Go through EVERY category within the More Demographics option in order to familiarize yourself with your filtering options.

Understand that the more sought-after your target audience, the more expensive your advertisement will be. For example, it is easy to want to target individuals who earn more than $125k a year or who are worth more than $2 million because they likely can afford your product. However, because those options are the highest income/net worth category options on Facebook, selecting these options instantly will put you in direct competition with luxury brands and services that are willing to pay lots of money to have these high value potential customers see their advertisements.

We will often try to come up with creative ways of targeting these groups of people without using identical filters. I'll give you an example as we go through the next section: Interests.

Interests give us a new box once more: this time, a Suggestions element is grayed out:

If you absolutely know there is something specific in which your target audience is interested (for example, if I am Rolex, my audience might be interested in "luxury watches" and various types of "Rolex" watches) you can type it directly into the box. If you are unsure or simply want to find more interests, you'll want to hit the browse button and go through every category once again. Seriously, please take the time right now to go through every category within interests.

Facebook is smart and provides suggestions based on of what interests you've already selected. Let's pretend you are coming out with a forensic science game and you want to target people who watch CSI on television. Type CSI into the box and select "CSI: Crime Scene Investigation." You'll now notice that additional suggestions automatically have emerged (or click the suggestions button if they have not):

Sweet. From this list, I would select CSI: Miami, CSI: NY, and maybe NCIS (TV Series). I wouldn't select the other shows because they aren't closely enough related. Select those three and take a look at the Potential Audience:

You'll notice that Facebook has listed the interests we've chosen as an OR (our ad will be served to anyone who likes CSI: Crime Scene Investigation, CSI: Miami, CSI: NY, *OR* NCIS (TV Series). This "or" is the reason you need to make sure your targeting is hyper-focused. For example, if I wanted to target people who like the *Sherlock Holmes* movies, they might not *also* like CSI/NCIS, but they would still be served with an ad. Those people would not convert and we would waste money.

The next major targeting element is "Behaviors." Go through EVERY category within behaviors and make sure to stick to your ideal audience. You likely will discover new elements of your ideal audience that you didn't write out before – add them to your list.

You can hover your mouse over any category that you have selected or are considering choosing and Facebook will provide a summary of what makes up that category as well as how many people on Facebook fit that category:

We use Behaviors and Interests to come up with creative targeting. For example, I once ran an advertisement campaign that targeted wedding photographers. There is no "wedding photographer" Job Title from which to choose. I couldn't select photography as an interest because that would be too broad and general. And, as always, I want to try to filter for an audience that is prepared to spend money.

I looked up the latest and greatest cameras online. There were maybe 5-7 made by Nikon and Canon that were quite expensive. I added those cameras under interests, which effectively filtered by audience for "people who are either passionate about high-end cameras or who likely own them." In other words, people who have likely spent lots of money on an expensive camera. I then targeted "Small Business Owners" under Behaviors. Through this combination, I had found photographers who own their own photography business and care enough about the quality of their shots to spend money on cameras (a small portion of this group definitely would be business owners who randomly/as a hobby are into photography, but the overwhelming majority is exactly what I am seeking). I then used the copy in the ad to target wedding photographers specifically.

That last paragraph is an example of the power of combining everything you've learned thus far in this book. It's about whom your audience is, and knowing as much as possible about it. It's about understanding the tools of the Facebook advertising platform, as well as the importance and theory behind the messaging of your advertisements. You cannot lose if you apply everything you are learning.

But, I digress...

Check out your potential audience once more. I generally keep campaigns targeted to under 100,000-200,000 people (although I've run campaigns to fewer than 1,000 people and more than 2 million people, so the rule of thumb is that there is no rule of thumb).

If you are just starting, I would suggest segmenting your audience to around 10,000 people, because the higher level of filtration will allow your ROI to be greater. Just keep in mind that it will take longer for you to reach your campaign goals because the potential audience is a metric for 30 days of advertising.

Chapter 8 Avoid being banned from advertising on Facebook

If you plan to use Facebook for advertising and making money, it is very important to know when enough is enough. As we discussed earlier, Facebook prides itself on the ability to protect subscribers from excessive advertisement. Their subscribers use the service to connect with family and friends, not to be bombarded with commercials they see through all other sources of media. While the advertisement is allowed, it is Facebook's policy to stop pages who overutilize this service from using their website. Yes, that means your page can be banned from Facebook if all you do is advertise.

Once you cross this line, it is nearly impossible to get your page reactivated. Clearly, you will have worked quite a bit to develop and promote your page, so losing it all together can be devastating, especially if it is a source of income. Rather than beg for forgiveness and the rights to your page, which is usually unsuccessful, avoid being banned in the first place.

There are a few easy rules to follow to keep this from happening. In general, Facebook flags sites that promote online dating and singles matching. Having seen these come up in several emails, it is obvious some pages sneak by for a while, but will swiftly end up in the dumpster. If your business is matchmaking, be clear as to the intentions of your business, and avoid coming across as pushy.

Keep your content fresh, as multiple accounts of the same post are a red flag as well. If the majority of your site are combinations of the same ads over and over, your account will be flagged. Also, if it appears that you have made a Facebook account for the sole purpose of selling advertising space, your account will likely be shut down. Facebook considers this "spamming" or creating digital junk mail. Nobody likes that, not even Facebook.

Posting copyrighted content from other websites is a red flag as well. Just because the content is readily accessible online does not mean that you can pass that info off as your own. If you do want to bring attention to someone else's work, make sure they get the credit. The courtesies we learned in high school English regarding siting references has been extended to the internet, but honestly, it couldn't be simpler. If you want to site an article, simply copy and paste the URL of the page where the article is found. Not only can your viewers see the full article, but it will also provide the website on your post showing where you found the information.

Common sense prevails here. We have already discussed how creating beneficial, real content that helps your target audience is the best way to build organic traffic. It is also the key to maintaining your website and not getting shut down. Yes, it is okay to promote your website and advertise for other companies, but do it with integrity, much like you would run the business. Make sure the majority of your posts are coming directly from your business, not other companies. Create new and interesting content that will intrigue viewers, causing them to like and share organically, not forced by ads.

In the process of creating your page, make sure not to mislead your viewers. There are some gross examples of misuse, like giving the impression you are a non-profit organization out to save cats and dogs, but run a kill shelter. That's pretty awful, but this is a crazy world we live in, and people will do just about anything to drive traffic to their pages. Avoid doing this by following your conscience and representing yourself and your business in a way that reflects your mission statement. Any legitimate business owner should already have this code of ethics under their belt.

If you are unsure whether or not your marketing ideas fit into Facebook guidelines consult with the page guidelines. Simply do a search for Facebook guidelines in your search bar or on any search engine. Here you will find a full list of terms and conditions of use. If you still are not sure, use the Facebook help desk forum to ask questions.

Chapter 9 Content Marketing in Facebook

I'm sure you know by now, but besides ease of communication with friends and family, Facebook offers a platform for sharing various kinds of content. The content on Facebook also serves a variety of purposes. People share things with the aim of news reporting, exchange of information, or simply entertainment, but the content on Facebook is often used for marketing goals as well – and successfully so.

As with any platform on the web, content marketing is an effective strategy for Facebook. It is one of the best ways to get people's attention. On Facebook, there are four types of content: text, video, images and links. Before preparing any type of content, you should become familiar with how each type of content is shown in your newsfeeds. Let's take a look.

Pure Text Content

Text contents take up the least amount of space and are probably the least engaging of the four types of content mentioned above. Facebook feeds are very busy. There are many other elements in various feeds much more likely to grab your target user's attention than pure text. The only types of text contents that consistently get attention are rants and emotional statements and these are not what you're interested in.

By large, people prefer to look at images or watch videos. For the average user, there is a lot of content to shuffle through when they visit their Facebook homepage. Upon seeing a post with a lot of text and no image or video, most people will only read the first sentence or two (if even that) before scrolling further down. On its own, textual content will work if it's exceptionally interesting or concise and grabs the reader's attention right away. Otherwise, it is important to combine it with something else that will attract the average user.

When a person sees an interesting image or video on Facebook, they are much more likely to read the text that accompanies it, so make sure that it relates and offers valuable background information on what they just saw.

Using text effectively as part of your content marketing strategy means employing economical language. It can also mean telling a story. As always, humor appeals to Facebook users, especially when combined with a unique graphic or interesting video. As a matter of fact, there's hardly a better way of reaching people than through humor. If you can make someone laugh, you can make them do all sorts of other things, least of which are sharing, liking and otherwise reacting to your content.

Whatever the story is, ensure that the punch line is arrived at soon and further, that it's supporting your brand. A customer endorsement, a success story, or promotional text should be upbeat, well-written and deliver maximum impact in as few words as possible.

Avoid the use of exclamation points as a substitute for saying something that's actually exciting. The overuse of exclamation points is a sign that you're unable to craft a message effectively. They appear unprofessional and even overwrought. Just! Say! No! to exclamation points, unless they're genuinely called for.

Just adding exclamation points into otherwise regular text is but a poor attempt to manipulate your reader's response. Unless the text has substance and really strikes a chord with the user, the chances are that they won't share your enthusiasm and will find your style of writing silly and coming across as trying too hard.

Images

Adding a compelling image is the best way to provoke engagement with your content. High quality images with positive messaging appeal to almost all users of Facebook.

The thing about images is that they are always to the point and are the most concise and impactful content you can find. Viewing them takes a matter of seconds, and they are usually the most shared type of content out there. You'll almost always find that successful pages make frequent use of images to promote their products and punctuate their points when posting text.

Adding an image also increases your content's presence, as images command more space on the feeds of other users. As stated earlier, visual content is one of the most important features of successful feeds on Facebook and can radically improve your user engagement.

While a piece of text blends into the Facebook homepage and is easily overlooked, images immediately garner attention. It's not just about the fact that they take up more space, it's also about their power of delivering a message. If you are the creator of your visual content, try to make clever use of coloring schemes to attract attention even easier. Bright colors and adequate combinations of colors will occupy just about anybody's mind. Strong reactions to certain colors are in our very nature, and they have been used by the advertising industry for ages.

Using software to create your own images is perhaps more time-consuming than sharing existing graphics, pulled from other online sources. But taking this step is another important support for your brand. You control the imagery. You control the imagery's message and you build your brand at the same time. A bonus? You place your logo on the images you create and a message that further supports your brand. This is good practice and creating your own images is a skill you should either develop or one you might enlist someone else to do on your behalf.

Depending on the level of development of your page and your financial means, you can hire the services of illustrators and freelancers for this purpose. There are plenty of people online who are very skillful in Photoshop or Adobe Illustrator, and they make a living by producing visual content for clients. If you don't know any such people personally, you can turn to freelance websites where countless artists offer their services. Freelancer and Upwork are among such sites, and they get millions of projects assigned and done on a regular basis.

There are many rich sources for images online, one of which is Pinterest. Positive, motivational, supportive messages, for example, are very effective on Monday mornings. A message with a picture of a beach, wishing your followers a relaxing weekend might be just the ticket on a Friday. High quality images (those which are landscaped and "tabloid" size work best on Facebook) that speak to your followers are what you're looking for. There are millions out there. Use them as brand support and to boost your engagement.

Videos

Videos are the most popular of the four types of content. By uploading a video to your page, you are inviting people to enjoy a show, basically. Videos are known to boost engagement almost exponentially, particularly when they're self-produced (something you can do on your mobile device or digital camera), humorous, or based on a universal theme (peace, family, etc.).

The appeal of videos is due to a number of factors. One of those factors, again, is the fact that there is no reading to be done. Although videos require more attention than a still image, people definitely love to watch interesting ones. Videos are also a great way for people to connect as they often feature things that a lot of people have in common, making them the most relatable form of content out there probably.

The ability of Facebook videos to grab follower attention has also improved because of the auto-play feature recently implemented by Facebook. As with Instagram, the auto-play feature activates the video when you scroll onto it in your newsfeeds. Automatically, a short clip of the video posted plays without the sound.

In a moment of pure genius, someone came up with the idea of making videos play automatically on websites. This means that people will see them as they would Gif files while scrolling through their feeds. Moving pictures immediately draw people's attention much more effectively than a simple thumbnail and are very likely to make users click on them to see the full thing. Users can still disable this option on Facebook, but most of them won't bother as their playback without audio is hardly an annoyance.

Your followers will be able to see the entire video, with audio, if they click on it. During the first few months of implementation, this feature increased engagement by Facebook users exponentially and has also increased the number of videos uploaded to Facebook every day. In fact, Facebook's video engagements doubled almost overnight. The Wall Street Journal reports that 88% of top content sites on the internet now use this feature, following the success of its implementation at Facebook.

Links

Links are the only types of content that will make your followers leave Facebook. There are three parts of a link's content involved, when these are shared to Facebook. The top portion is the description (pure text content), where you can add a personal message to your followers. This is where you can put some of your humor and creativity to use to attract more attention. It's where you place your pitch and make people interested in following your link in your own words. It's important to keep the description short and to the point, especially if the link already leads to a place where there is text to be read.

Just below it, you will see the link's preview. The preview includes a featured image and a small text area that contains the title and an excerpt of the text on the landing page. If the link leads to an article, for example, the preview will feature the title of that article, as well as the first sentence or two, giving Facebook users a glimpse into what they would read if they followed the link.

If you are trying to build an audience and get more page likes, you need to share the type of content that encourages people to take further action and follow the link you're posting. That includes offering informative text that encourages them to do so, possibly with an excerpt from the content at the link. Replacing an image from the landing page with something you feel is more evocative of the content on offer, or an entertaining video can also spur user action. Building on content in this way is great for encouraging engagement in the form of likes, shares and comments.

Remember that every single post you make and every step you take on Facebook is a new opportunity to bolster your promotional efforts and advance your relationship with the followers of the page. Approach each post as a piece of its own and give it utmost consideration as every time you post, you further consolidate your page or brand.

If your goal is to provoke certain actions by your followers, compelling them to venture outside the realm of Facebook, then you need to make effective use of links. This means supporting them with the addition of text and images that make them curious enough to take those actions.

The chances are that your followers will trust you enough to visit the links you post without thinking too much about it or being suspicious. However, there are other reasons not to visit the links posted on Facebook. Lack of interest or reason to visit the link will probably be leading cause of poor traffic. Don't underestimate the laziness of people when they are spending their leisure time browsing Facebook.

General Guidelines for Effective Facebook Content Marketing

The biggest challenge for most Facebook page managers is how to consistently create great content. If your business already has a website where you place all your content, then you only need to duplicate your actions there and perhaps customize it to appeal to your audience at Facebook.

A thing to keep in mind is that the bigger your following gets, the more content of ever increasing quality you'll need to put out to meet the demand and keep your followers interested. As your page grows, a time will come when you should begin to consider teaming up with other pages and content creators to fill up your own page with what they are producing. Having a large base is a powerful advantage that you can leverage to get more content, as smaller pages that may have good quality stuff but lack the followers will jump at the opportunity to be promoted by you.

1. Choose a goal

Before creating any form of content, you should write down your business goals for the week or the month of content marketing. Who do you want to reach? Do you want to drive traffic from Facebook to your website? If so, then see above and go beyond customization of your site's content. Offer something different for Facebook followers. Include links to key content on your web page and a call-to-action that provides your followers with a direct portal to get there.

It's also important to map out when you want to release certain content, time your posting right and form a schedule to adhere to. All good managers are highly organized and have a keen sense of timing. That's where you begin to plan out your week or month. Be considerate of any possible holidays, specific days of the week, etc. If you come up with too many goals, make use of Facebook's tools for scheduling posts to show up automatically at a given time and on a particular date.

2.   Identify the type of content that you should use

Choose the appropriate types of content for the goal you've set. If you're hoping to raise brand awareness, then using a combination of imagery and video content with occasional text/link content is your best bet. What is the story you're telling and who are you telling it to? What do they want to see? These questions should be at the front of your mind when identifying the type of content that serves you best on Facebook.

Knowing your business is the first step towards representing it well. You have to know perfectly well what it is that you are doing, what you intend to do in the future, and where you want to take your enterprise. The second crucial step is knowing your market and your followers on Facebook. Marketing is a two-way street, and you won't succeed by just putting out content for the sake of putting out content. It's paramount that you constantly observe your audience and their reactions to your posts. Be mindful of what makes them laugh, sets them off, and what produces the most user engagement. Always adjust your content to the requirements of the market and be ready to reconsider the ideas you may have had before, as you may sometimes find that what you thought would cause a significant reaction was actually met dissatisfaction.

3.   Produce quality content

Image-based content is easy to find online. Your goal, though, is to ensure it's of high quality and relevant to your brand's mission. Further, it must be compelling enough to engage your followers. As said above, though, creating your own image-based content is by far the more effective strategy. You are in control. Often, you'll find you need to create your own images, as you can't find quite what you're looking for elsewhere. It's worth the time and effort to brand yourself effectively and maintain control of your message.

Once again, it may be a good idea to seek professional assistance if you have the monetary means for that. Make use of someone else's proficiency in visual design software and get original, quality content tailored to your specific needs, without putting any of your own time into it. If you don't have the money but have the time, though, there are many good courses and tutorials online, paid and free, which you can use to learn these skills for yourself and produce completely original content by your own hand.

The same goes for video content. However, videos don't just require a camera; there is also editing that goes into the job, or even effects if the situation demands it. This is, again, all something that you can do on your own if you have the skills, the time, and the tools, but it may prove harder than expected. The power of today's software definitely facilitates such processes like never before, but it's still a skill to be mastered. Luckily, there are plenty of freelance editors and video creators out there who excel at such tasks and offer their services for a fixed or hourly rate. If you need animation, you can arrange that too. The only limitation is your budget. Videos are sometimes hard to make if you want quality production, though, and it is very important that they are visually appealing and smooth for the viewer.

Quality videos are more difficult to create on your own. Posting low quality or pixelated videos may hurt your page's reputation rather than improve it. But in this age of top notch mobile device technology, it's likely you're up to the challenge. Trial and error will tell you if the videos you provide yourself are going to work for you. If you have a big marketing budget, then you can have videos made for your Facebook page. You should need to ensure, however, that those videos would help you reach your Facebook marketing goals. Otherwise, all your video making efforts will be for nothing. Again, examining what competitors have done in this area is useful.

Linking your Facebook page to your website or blog is an effective way of spreading the gospel of what you're selling. Your site or blog should feature a varied content mix that's exciting to visit, because it's well maintained and not static. There's nothing worse than sending followers to your website and having them discover it hasn't been updated for weeks. This will turn them off in a hurry. Keep your content fresh and evolving. You should then share your website to Facebook by either posting the link in your page's status bar or by using your website's share-to-Facebook feature. Don't forget to include compelling text content to encourage your followers to click on the link. Driving two way traffic between Facebook and the other web presences of your brand will grow your online identity.

4. Optimize your posts for maximum engagement

Facebook allows page managers to add a short description to all the content types they share. Aside from auto-playing videos, these descriptions are probably the most attention-grabbing element of any post. People look at this factor when they become interested in viewing the video, image or link that you've share.

Users will want to know the gist of the content before deciding whether or not they want to give it a more thorough look. That's why your description needs not only to be concise, but very descriptive and easily understood. Always aim to provide as much information as possible, while keeping the number of words in the description to an absolute minimum.

You need to make sure your description uses the kind of language your target audience usually sees in their feeds. Posting questions and emotional statements in the description is also effective in gathering engagement. Humor is another useful tool for user engagement, when carefully choosing your words to introduce your content.

Funny content is likely at the very top when it comes to sharing. People just love a laugh or a chuckle, and they will make sure to share that with their friends, who may share it even further. Another type of content that generates a lot of sharing is shocking content, and I mean that in the most general sense, but these kinds of stunts should be avoided as they are more risky. You can never go wrong with a fair amount of humor, though.

Including a headline in your content is another effective strategy for catching user attention. Facebook usually posts the page titles of links when they're shared. If you're using links to direct traffic to your website, then you need to make sure you optimize the page title to encourage clicks on your links. An effective format to encourage this action is adding a word that suggests further action by the user. Examples of words like these are "click", "visit", "look", or "check out". Take a look at the call-to-action words your competitor pages use. What's working there? What's not? Encouraging engagement with the use of language that invites an interactive relationship with your users can be a very effective means of boosting your presence. It also brings users into a two way communication with you and your brand. You invite. They take up the invitation.

It may sound overly simplistic and too direct to yield a result, but it usually does work. A word as simple as "click" urges immediate action and can be surprisingly impactful. Sometimes the simplest way to make someone do something is just to ask them to, and the internet is full of examples where this simple principle happens to work.

You can also add a headline to images and videos. For images, you can do this by adding text at the top of the image, using image manipulation software like Photoshop or GIMP. This strategy works well with videos, because the auto-play features doesn't provide audio, as we discussed earlier.

Measure Effectiveness

If your content is fully optimized to help you reach your goals, then you need to find a way to measure its effectiveness. Some goals can be measured using the insights feature of the Facebook page. If your goal includes actions outside the network, you may need to use data gathering tools like Google Analytics to measure your campaign's success.

As we will discuss a little later on in this book, Facebook offers a few tools to help you monitor the impact of your marketing campaign. You can track all kinds of actions like clicks, likes, views, registrations, checkouts, shares, etc. These tools can be used to get deeper insight into the efficiency of both your Facebook page and your other websites that you manage and promote over Facebook ads.

- Experiment with possible improvements

No marketing campaign is perfect. There are always some areas in need of improvement. The best features of your content and ad campaigns will change as your page audience and your marketing goals change. Experiment with your strategy, tweaking as you go. The online world is dynamic and volatile. You need to remain sensitive to that and nimble enough to shift your focus.

Your targeted market is a living, breathing thing that reacts to many different forces like trends and new social climates, and your page or site will need some work until it becomes influential. Regardless of your influence, the market will always tell you what you are doing right and what needs to change. You just have to read the signs and pay attention, while always ready to change habits and alter your approach as the people demand.

Chapter 10 Facebook Sales Funnel

Facebook is no longer just the coolest social media platforms on the busy web; it is no longer just another place for teens to share their updates with their friends; it is bigger than ever before. It is growing every day and is not likely to slow down in the near future. This is a good news for advertisers as the marketing opportunities it offers are immense. You can increase engagement with your potential customers, you can create and build brand awareness, you can make conversions, and increase sales. It all depends on what your ad objectives are and what you want to accomplish using this powerful platform. Facebook has more to do with socializing than anything else. In most cases, making a purchase would be the last thing on anybody's mind while browsing through the News Feed on Facebook, which means the possibility of selling on this platform is less. This is the reason why many brands become disappointed trying to sell their products on Facebook. They might be getting more engagement and more followers but still not be able to achieve their ad objective of increasing sales. The problem is not with the platform, it is the approach these advertisers take by trying to sell things to someone who might not even be interested. They should understand they cannot sell something to a user who doesn't have the purchasing mindset.

So, if you see an opportunity, it doesn't mean it is an opportunity to sell your product. This also doesn't mean that no one goes to Facebook with buying on their mind. Hence, you need to find the right set of people who might be interested in what you are offering. The best way of doing it is by developing a sales funnel.

Creating a Facebook Sales Funnel

Step #1: Create catchy and relevant content

To build a sales funnel, the first thing you need is different forms of content – video, blogs, webinars, ebooks, and so on. Different forms are required so that you can reach different types of audiences; some of them are more into watching the video, some like reading blog posts, so ensure you cater to different types of audiences. It is always good to have a good variety so that you have something for all sub-niche categories of your target audience. The content that you choose to put on your website to drive sales should be high quality and relevant to what you want to sell. Once your content reaches them, they are part of your funnel.

Step #2: Promote content to only those who are interested – a warm audience

Once you have the relevant content for your target audience, ensure it reaches the right set of people who are "warm". A warm audience means people who already know about you and your brand, and have shown some sort of interest in it. They can be your Facebook fans or a part of your website retargeting list. Regardless, ensure you engage with them and try to find out what is it that helps you make sales. Also, if you see that your warm audience is responding well to your content, there are chances that even a cold audience will. Therefore, analyze the data you get and see what's working and what's not.

Step #3: Do not forget to target your Lookalike Audience

Facebook gives you an opportunity to create Lookalike Audience – these are those who are very similar to your existing customers in terms of habits, interests, and behaviors. Hence, you can consider them as a cold audience who can be warmed easily since they look like the warm audience. To target them, navigate to the 'Audiences' section of your ads and then click on 'Create a Lookalike Audience'. You can find people who are similar to your most valuable targets. Select Source – which can be a Page, a conversion tracking Pixel or a Custom Audience. Next, select a Location and then Audience Size that can range anywhere from 1 to 10 percent of the total population in the locations you selected. Remember the smaller the percentage, the closer the match to your existing audience will be. Once done, click on 'Create Audience'.

Step #4: Advertise what is the best

The content that was most liked by your warm audience is the best content. You must take it to the cold audience to see if it can warm them too. The content can be in any form – it can be videos, blogs, or ebooks. The goal should be to move at least a part of the cold audience into your sales funnel so that they are aware of your brand. Only when they turn into a warm audience will they consider making a purchase. Without awareness, there cannot be a purchase.

Step #5: Consider remarketing to convert part of the cold audience into a warm audience

As we discussed previously, Facebook is more about socializing than purchasing. Most of the people are connecting with others and rarely do they consider making a purchase on this platform. This doesn't mean you cannot consider Facebook to help you in selling your products. With Facebook advertising, you cannot expect a cold audience to directly transform into qualified leads as this is not how it works on Facebook. Only when the cold audience is exposed to a brand multiple times, will they think about making a purchase. You can expose them to your brand several times so that they become a part of your funnel by remarketing.

Step #6: Using various options for remarketing

Utilize the power of Facebook Pixel: A powerful feature of Facebook advertising is Pixel that helps you remarket so that the user comes back to you to complete the purchase.

Use the power of visuals: Apart from Pixel, there are several other techniques that can be used for remarketing and one of the best ones is Videos. As we know visuals are more impactful, they can help you expose your brand to the audience.

Step #7: Create more warmth for your leads

With the help of remarketing, you could add some of your audience to the sales funnel. This is a great news but we need to do more than just this. This way you are only addressing a part of your audience as not everyone will convert. For example, perhaps some of the users visited your site and downloaded the free ebook but they never bought a copy from your website. To resolve this issue, create and run an ad to explain the benefits of what you are offering so that they are convinced.

Facebook Landing Page

The number of 'Likes' on your post and all the traffic you managed to generate with the help of News Feed ads are not worth much if you are not meeting the ad objective. To help you with this and to convert traffic into sales, advertisers are using a powerful marketing tool known as a Facebook Landing page. A Facebook Landing page is an independent webpage, which is standalone and not linked to the main navigation of your website. It is created so that users can take actions on your page. These actions could be signing up for your service, downloading a copy of your ebook, or buying the product from your website. Since it is designed in such a way to persuade the user to take an action, it is more convincing than any other page. But remember it is not just the design that attracts the users. To reap maximum benefits from the landing page, it should be in line with the advertising campaign it is part of, which means every promotion that you run would require its own unique page.

Why a business needs a landing page.

A landing page saves you from building your business on rented space. Think about where your business would be if Facebook and other social media platforms disappear tomorrow. Although it is very unlikely to happen if you are heavily dependent on a platform because your customers exist only there then your relationship with them is at stake. It is at the mercy of the next change in Facebook's working algorithm. Even if you don't think it this way, Facebook is a rented space and you do not own it the way you own your mailing list. By creating a landing page that gets all your fans onto the emailing lists, you have access to your customers beyond any social media platform. You can always connect with them and share updates about your new products through emails and add them to automated sequences to turn them into your potential customers. This way a Facebook Landing page offers you better opportunities to get your fans onto your emailing lists.

A landing page on Facebook can also help you achieve higher opt-in rates. The same landing page, when put on Facebook, is capable of earning more opt-ins. This is because people who visit your website do not know about you and there is less chance that they will respond to your lead generation campaigns. After all, people are not comfortable sharing their contact details with someone they do not know. On the other hand, they are well aware of Facebook and its credibility. They might even be seeing posts from you on a regular basis, and you might have even responded to some of their queries or comments on Facebook. So, they know your brand on Facebook and trust you enough to share their email address. Even if they have not interacted with you before, the element of trust attached to Facebook offers a certain level of credibility to your brand. Therefore, the landing pages get higher opt-in rates when they are published on a Facebook tab.

A Facebook Landing page is a perfect place to publish your ads. When the traffic is diverted to a Facebook tab, it is capable of achieving better approval rates. Hence, a landing page, when published on the custom Facebook tab, performs better.

Attributes of an Effective Facebook Landing Page

For a Facebook Landing page to be effective, it should have these attributes –

- *No Body, Footer or Outbound Links.* If there is nobody, footer or an outbound navigation link, it is difficult for a user to escape your website without converting. Instead of clicking on other tabs or links, he will remain focused on the Call-to-action. They do not have to leave the website to know more about you. Due to the same reasons, you should avoid having other pages, such as 'Careers', 'Contact Us' and so on. The logo on the page should take the users to the Home page. However, the focus for the user should be the Call-to-action.

- *A headline that speaks for itself.* Telling the world about the benefits your product offer isn't easy and that's why there are professionals who do this for business owners. The focus of the website and its design should always be such that the users know why they should approach you and how are you better than competitors. The first thing that appears on the landing page is the header. Therefore, ensure it is something that speaks to the benefits of your product.

- *A strong message that tells them they are in the right place.* Your landing page should have a strong message to the users that they are in the right place. It's the reason the Facebook Ad drives them to the landing page. This is called "message match" and is helpful in building trust with the user. The landing page's colors, headline, and everything else that the user sees should be in line with the ad.

- *Content that shows the benefits of the product.* Always bear your target audience in mind while you are curating content for your landing page. Remember that the readers are busy people and might not be interested in something that is complicated and sophisticated. They might not spend much time on your page. This is an opportunity to help them evaluate your offer. You might have an excellent vocabulary, but this is not the place to show off. Be as natural as possible so it sounds genuine. Don't get poetic - use bullet points to highlight the benefits of your product. Design it so it is easy for the user to skim through the content as that's all they can afford to do given the time limits. Note that bullet points are capable of enticing them to read what's given. If there is a long text, they might find the design too busy to read.

- *Visuals that help them connect with you.* Because visuals speak louder than words and are capable of conveying the underlying message efficiently and quickly, videos and images are always given preferences over text on the landing pages. These visuals are particularly useful in cases where a lot of information needs to be added – sales page and click-through landing pages. This is because explainer videos and infographics can effectively replace text that makes the pages content heavy. They also help the users understand your offering in a more effective and precise way.

- *Social proof yields more traffic.* Humans generally go by the recommendations of others who have tried something before. If there is good rating given to a hotel, we are more likely to try it. If there is always a queue outside a café, we assume it serves very good coffee. If your friend tells you that a particular movie is good, you'll want to see it. These are examples of social proof. You can use testimonials from your customers to prove that your product adds value. Buttons and widgets that provide information about the number of people who like your page can help users to know that your business has a good following. You can also showcase some of the things you have done in the past to boost traffic on your landing page. Buyers take cues from others. According to a survey conducted, approximately 88% of the users consider the online reviews of the product that other buyers have posted.

- *Catchy 'Call-to-action'.* The Call-to-action is the most important attribute of your landing page. Without this, a user cannot convert. Always include a button that is capable of getting the attention of visitors and motivate them to make purchase decisions. Also, the page should show the benefits of the offering over the features. For example – if the objective is to make people sign up for a class that can help them get a job in the foreign country, include an appropriate button. Do not include 'register' or 'download'. Try to use something that encourages them to click.

These features make your landing page effective, but there is always room for improvement on the first cut of your landing page. You can always learn new things that you can incorporate to make it even more efficient. For instance – the headline can be more optimized to resonate with the requirements of the users or the copy can be search engine optimized. One of the easiest and efficient ways to know that can be improved on your Facebook Landing page is the A/B method of testing.

A/B testing, also known as split testing, refers to a testing mechanism that compares two different landing pages at the same time – one is the 'A' version and another one is the 'B' version. Everything else remains the same including campaign run times, traffic sources and so on. It is a tactic by which you can find out which Call-to-action, ad headline, images, or body copy works best for your target audience. You can try out different ad placements and Facebook audiences to see which one is the perfect choice and where they are. There are two ways you can use the A/B to test your landing page.

One of the myths around A/B test is that you can only test one attribute at a time. For instance, to determine how effective the headline of the landing page is, you can compare the original page that has the headline to be tested against a variation of that page with a different heading. Whichever of these can attract and convert more visitors has the better and more effective headline.

This is the most accurate way to compare two pages, but it is certainly not the only one. Sometimes it is not possible to compare just one attribute at a time due to the test duration. That's why when a complete redesign of the page is needed there is a need to test multiple attributes at the same time. The variation page is compared with the original page in terms of form, headline, and even featured images. Once the complete test runs, the one that attracts a higher conversion wins because the ultimate goal of having a good landing page is to generate more conversions. Why it is better is not really important.

The steps involved in the A/B test.

Step 1: Collect Data to Be Analyzed

Test your landing page only when you have a reason. For testing, you can use your website or any of the several tools available in the market to determine how your Custom Audience is behaving. With the help of Google Analytics, you can see if your customers are abandoning the landing page without even visiting it. If it's happening, you need to discover the underlying cause and action on it immediately. For instance, if people are clicking on the navigation bar of your landing page instead of clicking the Call-to-action button, it is good to remove these kinds of distractions so that people focus on the Call-to-action. Try hiding the navigation button and now compare the page with the original page. You will see a boost in your conversions.

Step 2: Determine how many visitors you have to your page

You need to determine the number of visitors in a way that has statistical significance. This means you need to know how many visitors you need on each of your pages to be confident it is the genuine number and not happening by chance. Most of the industries have 95% as the accepted statistical significance, which means this percentage gives you confidence that the test results can be attributed to changes you made to the landing page.

Step 3: Develop Your Variation Page

The step involves making changes to your landing page based on the results of your A/B test – changes that will boost the conversion rate. For example, if it is determined that making changes to the headline can attract more visitors, you can create a new test page with the new headline. Also, if the results showed there is a need to add an image, create the variation page with the new headline and added image. All the changes you make as part of variation page shouldn't affect the control page. This is important because, without a baseline, you cannot compare the control page to understand how the variation page will perform.

Step 4: Test the new elements and the existing functionality

Before running the test, some of the things you must check are:

- The links are working fine and ads are directing you to the correct page
- The form is giving the right information to the CRM system
- When users click on CTA buttons, they are directed to the 'thank you' page
- The landing page looks correct in all the browsers

Step 5: Drive More Traffic to Your Landing Page

Once everything is tested, you can start generating traffic to your landing page. With Facebook, you can test traffic coming from different sources – News Feed ads, sidebar ads, audience network, and from different segments – females, males, singles etc., to evaluate the impact of traffic from these sources on your conversion rate. Remember that you shouldn't end the test before it reaches at least 95% statistical significance.

Step 6: Analyze the test results and improvise the landing page

Look at the results you have collected from various sources to see if the variation you created could achieve what you were looking for. If not, repeat the same process again, and keep testing and making changes till you see the desired results.

The Four Golden Rules of A/B Testing Ads:

Rule 1: Test only one attribute or variable at a time because of the fewer the variables, the more accurate the results. Testing just one variable per experiment makes tracking easier.

Rule 2: Use the correct campaign structure for your Facebook ads. You have two options: A single test set where all the ad variations are in a single ad set, and multiple single variation ad sets where each of the variations is part of separate ad set. If you place all the variations in a single set, you will not be able to see the relevant test results. Therefore, it is recommended that you should use the multiple single variation ad sets where all the variations are tested separately.

Rule 3: Make sure the test results from the split test are valid. You tested your campaign and you have your results now. To test the authenticity of your split test, you will have a good amount of result data. You can also use A/B Significance Test to determine the authenticity of your test results.

Rule 4: Set a budget that is sufficient for the split test. You will need more advertising impressions as well as conversions if you are testing more ad variations. This will eat up your budget. Ensure you do not overdo it, but it should be just right so that you can get valid results.

Facebook Remarketing

Remarketing can be described as targeting the users who visited your website through an ad you had posted on Facebook. The platform gives advertisers an opportunity to show ads that resonate well with their content – whether it is about a blog post or about a product that they viewed. This requires creating ads and targeting website Custom Audiences.

The most important thing about advertising is targeting the right set of people, and remarketing helps you target those who showed interest in what you are offering. This is not the only factor that determines the success or failure of your ads, but it is by far the most important one. You can create the best copy with a great design and brilliant content, but if it doesn't reach the right set of people, what's the point of having the ad at all.

Chapter 11 How to Set up Facebook Business Manager

A lot of people tend to avoid using Facebook business manager because they believe that it is a complicated setup that will consume a lot of their time. One of the best things about the Facebook business manager is it actually helps you to save on a lot of time and, while the initial setup may seem complicated, once you've gone through it, you will be able to benefit from it long-term. Here is a detailed break-up of how you can set up your Facebook business manager by following the simple steps.

Create Your Facebook Business Manager Account

In order for you to create your Facebook business manager, you need to first create an account. In order for you to do this, you have got to go to business.Facebook.com and click on the create account big blue button which is at the left of the top of the screen. You then need to fill out all your information in the popup box and continue. Make sure that you enter your business email address to manage your business account and click finish once all these details are completed.

Add Your Business Page

This is really simple, and if you already have an existing Facebook page, you can automatically integrate it into your Facebook business page with a few steps. If you are trying to replicate your pages, you will need to grant access from your Facebook account to the business manager account in order for this to happen.

In order for you to do this, you need to go to the dashboard, click on add page, and click add page in the popup box again. If you have more than one account then make sure that you select the right one.

Add Your Facebook Ad Account

Once you get access to the existing Facebook page you can then request access to your Facebook ad account as well, which means if you have existing advertisements, you can control them using the business manager. On the business manager dashboard, once you click on add ad account you will also manage to get access to your ads manager. If you don't have an ad account on Facebook you can then create one in the business manager. In order for you to set up an ad account you have got to go back to the dashboard, click on the add ad account, and start creating your ad account. You need to enter all your details including an email address, payment method, and a little more information before the account is successfully set up.

Add People to Help Manage the Facebook Business Page

Marketing on Facebook is quite difficult, and if you are a large organisation and have multiple tasks at hand you can always hire a business manager to handle the page for you. You can add team members and also limit or restrict the amount of accessibility you want to give to them. There is a people and assets column in the business setting that you need to go to where you can assign assets to certain people and also grant how much access you would like them to have on the manager page itself.

Assign People to Manage Your Facebook Page

There are a number of assets that you would have on Facebook, and you need to be on top of your marketing efforts in order to be successful. In order to be in control of your Facebook marketing efforts, you need to add team members that can help take care of your Facebook business page and control your Facebook ad campaigns. This can be done through the business manager dashboard. When you are on the dashboard you need to click on business settings at the top of the page and then click on the people and assets tab. Under this tab you need to select people and this will show you a list of people that can access your Facebook business manager. If you have not added anybody then you will only see your name and the address list. You can then start adding team members and assign privileges to each of the team members. You can add a number of people depending on their responsibility. This includes freelance writers, employees, and business partners. This step only involves adding individuals to your Facebook business account. Once you have set the privileges for each of the team members, you then need to click on add people and move to the next section.

Next, you need to decide which of your team members have access to which part of the business page. Some people would have access only to the advertising page while others will have complete control as a moderator. Once you have assigned responsibilities to them, each of your team members will receive an email regarding the same. They need to accept the invitation in order to become a part of the Facebook business page. You need to inform your team members in advance that they could receive an email and they should accept the invitation immediately.

Link to Your Instagram Account

Instagram is an important social media channel and linking it to your Facebook account will give you more outreach. This can be done again under the people and assets tab and then you need to click on add Instagram account. You will then be asked to enter the credentials for your Instagram account. Once you enter that information you need to click next. The next steps will ask you if you have more than one account for your business and you can enter that account information as well.

Now that you have your business manager running, you need to access your dashboard where you can control all the activities for your Facebook business page. Apart from doing the above you also need to go ahead and set up Facebook pixels that will allow you to take your Facebook advertisement to the next level.

Setting Up Facebook Pixels

Facebook pixels is a coding that Facebook will help generate for you. When you enter this code on your website it will give access to information such as optimising Facebook ads and tracking conversion through your website. Facebook pixels is very helpful and it should be set up even before you start your first ad campaign. Under the people and assets tab you need to select pixels and then click on add. You don't need to give a name for your Facebook pixel account and click on create. On the next page you have the option of setting up your pixel now and once you click on next, your pixel will be generated. You can create up to 10 pixels for your account and you can use this to your advantage.

Placing Your Ad

When you are on the Facebook business manager dashboard you need to click on business manager that is at the top left hand side. When you click that, you need to click on create and manage and click on the create button. If you are doing this for the first time, you can select guided creation which will help you set up your campaign objective as well as select your target audience and your budget. Here you will be able to select your schedule for your ads and, when you click on save, you are ready for your first ad to go live. When you follow all the steps correctly you will be set to start your Facebook marketing campaign today.

Reasons You Should Be Advertising on Facebook

There is no denying that social media is definitely ruling the market when it comes to promoting your business online which is why it is very important for you to select the right platform for your business to grow. Facebook is still the best social media platform you can select because it has the highest number of active users and people tend to check Facebook on a regular basis. If you decide that you want to go with social media marketing but you are not too sure why Facebook is the best then here are some things about Facebook advertising you should know about.

Your Audience Is On Facebook

There is no denying that the people who you want to target are available on Facebook and it's easy for you to touch base with them because you are able to easily filter out unnecessary people and limit your budget effectively.

Facebook Advertisements Are Cheaper

There is no denying that Facebook advertising is relatively cheaper in comparison to the other advertising platforms on social media. You can also use organic boosts to increase your fan base and customer reach, which helps you to generate customers without spending any money.

Facebook Targeting Capabilities

There are a number of advertising channels that you can target, however Facebook targeting is definitely the best. Facebook has a number of targeting capabilities and it includes demographics, interests, behavior, age range, connections, and locations. Each of these capabilities can be further expanded and you will be able to target a specific group with the help of Facebook.

Facebook Helps Convert Leads

Facebook is perfect when it comes to targeting customers that have already visited your website in the past. Irrespective of whether or not these leads became customers in the past, Facebook will keep remarketing to them based on their behavior online. A number of businesses have called this the social stalker. Facebook is capable of stalking all your potential leads and targeting them based on what they currently require. For example if a customer has been searching for laptops, Facebook will know about this and will promote your business if you are in the laptop business. Facebook will never promote your ad to a customer that has been looking for products that do not fall within your niche.

Get New Leads Easily

Facebook is the perfect platform where you will be able to generate new leads almost on a daily basis. Apart from being able to generate new leads, you can even clone these leads with a lookalike audience feature that Facebook has. This feature enables Facebook to target an audience that is similar to your current target audience but may vary on a couple of parameters. The likelihood of these people also being interested in your business is very high and this is something that only Facebook can do for you. Facebook's target lookalike audience is based on people that have downloaded apps similar to your business app.

Benefits of the Facebook Pixel

Facebook pixel is one of the most interesting add-on tools that Facebook gives you. It's essential to help you create an interesting and successful marketing strategy that works in your favor. If you haven't already started using Facebook pixel then here are a few reasons why it needs to be integrated into your advertisement today.

Understanding Your Audience Better

Facebook pixel provides you with detailed insight that helps you to determine who your existing customers are as well as who are the potential customers. It provides you with analytics that not only identify the browsing activity of people but also their purchasing activity.

Relevant Engagement

If you are in the e-commerce business and you are looking to talk with people who are relevant to your business using pixel is highly recommended. It uses behavioral targeting to identify people who are looking for services or businesses like yours so that you can get in touch with them faster or they can get in touch with you after they see your advertisement.

Identify Shopping Journeys

Facebook pixel will help you understand shoppers that take a long time when they are browsing through products. Pixel data will help you understand what each of the customer looks for when they are selecting a product and what is the one aspect that appeals to them before they make the purchase. For example, for customers shopping for a new pair of jeans there are a number of things that he or she could look for. Your pixel data will give you all this information and it will show you what features the customer is looking for in their pair of jeans. Once you know the kind of features that attract a customer, you will be able to customize your ads based on that.

Quick Shoppers

Similar to shoppers that take a long time to purchase things, Facebook pixel will also help you identify shoppers that are very quick in their decision-making. Such customers are very specific with their requirements and they make a decision within a matter of minutes. Based on your pixel data you will be able to customize ads for these customers and help them purchase very quickly. These customers are driven by a call to action and you need to make sure that your ad features that.

Shopping In Store

There are a number of customer that still prefer walking into a store and purchasing things rather than purchasing online. If you are a business that also has stores across a city or a country, you can use your Facebook ads to promote the stores. You can provide the store location as well as your operating hours along with all the pricing information that will help your audience make a decision.

Chapter 12 Choose The Best Advertising Option For Your Business on Facebook

Facebook advertising comes in a number of forms and you need to make sure that you pick the right advertising method based on your business. Irrespective of what product or service you deal in there is a Facebook option available for you. Here are a few Facebook ad templates that you can use along with some successful examples.

Video Ad

As the name suggests this is an ad that features a video and it will appear in the news feed for your potential users. You need to get as creative as possible with your video because it can help create a very positive impact on the audience. If you are into the food industry then you can show a video of a recipe being made and how it can benefit the users. You can also show gadgets that are featured in your video that can help make life easier in the kitchen. There are various kitchen hacks that you can share with your users in the form of a video and this is something that will definitely create a positive impact.

Photo Ad

Photo ads are generally useful for businesses that deal with products that can be seen. Photo ads are more effective in selling products rather than selling services.

Reach Ad

A reach ad helps with promoting a particular shop or a product in a local area. For example, if you are having a sale in your local store, you can give information to customers based in that area and also provide details regarding the store. This ad will not show up to people that do not live in that area and this is how your ad can reach the maximum number of people. Reach ads can have a lot of impact, however there is a very limited scope because it is only specific to a particular segment.

Offer Ad

An offer advertisement helps promote certain offers that your business is bringing up. This will help get more customers interested in your business and you will be able to reach a wider audience irrespective of whether they have been your customers or not in the past. This advertisement will be shown only two people that have shown an interest in a similar product or service as yours. A classic example is if you are a local business that caters to pest control and if a customer has searched for pest control via a search engine, your Facebook ad will show up in the news feed of that particular customer. When you combine this targeting along with an offer ad, there is a very good chance that you will be able to convert a lead into a customer.

Event Ad

An event ad is very useful when it comes to promoting events in certain localities or even in certain cities. The event ad will give information regarding the event along with the timings. The event ad also ensures that you reach maximum people and you gain maximum participation for your event. Event ads will only be shown to people that have shown an interest in similar events in the past.

Retargeting Ad

Retargeting ad is a generic ad that will help target customers that have shown an interest in your business or are currently contemplating purchasing a product similar to your product. If a customer looks for restaurant listings in his or her area and you are a local restaurant that has newly opened, your ad will appear to this customer and you will be able to get them to eat in your restaurant. In order for your ad to be successful you need to have certain offers that may interest the customer. You will need to do proper research and prepare your ad based on what customers are looking for.

Targeting Based On The Audience

Facebook is available across multiple platforms and multiple operating systems. This means that every gadget that you have can be used to access Facebook and this makes it easier for you to reach a wider audience. However, you need to make sure that the format is correct irrespective of how the customer is viewing your ad.

Desktop / Laptop

If a customer is accessing Facebook from his or her desktop or laptop, then you will need to showcase your ads in a more traditional format. There are two ways it can showcase your ad to customers. You can choose to display ads on the right side of the screen. This ad will not interfere with the customer's newsfeed and it will be visible to the customer even if he or she keeps scrolling. The other way that you can display your ad on a laptop or a desktop is in the middle of the news feed. While this ad can grab attention, it can also get annoying if the customer keeps seeing your ad again and again. You need to make sure that you are selecting the right criteria for displaying your ads otherwise your ad may be marked as spam if it is being shown to the wrong user.

Mobile User

Almost 90% of all Facebook users access Facebook from their mobile phones. This means that you need to focus on creating the right mobile format for your ads so that the customer does not miss out on the ad and the visual experience is not hampered as well. When a customer is accessing Facebook through their mobile phone the ad will appear in the news feed and you need to make sure that you create the right ad because mobile phone users generally scroll by very quickly. If something does not catch their eye, they will not stop scrolling and you lose your chance of impressing and gaining a customer.

Chapter 13 How To Use Facebook Like A Pro For Your Business

Optimizing Content

Content refers to everything you post on your business page for your followers to see. Many businesses post photos and videos as well as text, since these are the most popular forms of content. Content can make or break a page. You'll need to know what to use and how to most effectively represent it as content.

There are four key tips to remember when choosing the best content:

1. The content of your business page must be relevant and reflect what your business does and the values it upholds.

2. Your content must be consistent in quality and style, regardless of the medium you use. Consumers put a high value on consistency and have come to expect the highest level of quality in the sites they visit. Your standards must be very high indeed.

3. Your content must motivate customers to engage with your business, going from first-time visitor, to regular reader, to loyal repeat customer.

4. Your content needs to appeal to your target audience, making them want to participate as a regular reader of your posts. First, you need to determine what you have done to encourage readers to like your page. Then you'll want to provide them with high-quality target information that applies to those interests.

Do people like your page because you provide discount codes? Do they value the practical usefulness of the information you share? Regardless of the reason, consumers must receive something that they value in exchange for their participation on your Facebook business page. Find out what your target audience values and then work out ways to deliver it in the form of high-quality content.

Posts that are purely text can be incredibly powerful. Because of this, Facebook has launched an option where you post short text using a large font on colorful backgrounds. The larger-than-usual text, on top of vibrant colors and patterns, stands out above the normal chatter on a page.

The most powerful content for any Facebook business page are videos and photos. Adding these to your posts will not just make your post stand out but it will also make your post more shareable. The more your posts are shared, the larger will be your audience and the greater your potential income

Using Images

Posts that include photos are 20 percent more likely to create engagement than posts without images. If posts include a video, the likelihood of engagement jumps to 80 percent.

When you use pictures and videos on your Facebook business page, they must be of the best quality and the highest resolution. Decent quality content marks you as a professional and it will make your readers more likely to share your content than will images that are blurry or text riddled with typos.

You'll want to carefully select pictures for use in your *profile*, your *cover photo,* and your *timeline*. Facebook promotes and supports the use of three types of picture files:

- .png
- .jpg

- .gif

Pictures that you have taken using a camera are best saved in a .jpg format. Graphics that are computer-generated, such as your business logo, are best saved in .png or .gif format. When you add a picture to your business page, Facebook will compress it, so no matter how large the file, it will not slow down the speed at which your page loads. Because of this compression, it is important that you save your pictures in the highest resolution available to you. If you use low resolution images, the compression will cause them to appear grainy and of poor quality, a turn-off to your potential customers.

Your Cover Image

Your *cover photo* can have a full display size of 820x312 pixels with a minimum of 399x150 pixels. Facebook allows you to upload a single cover photo. When you are ready to upload your cover photo, simply click the camera button you'll find on the bottom right-hand side of your top banner. Since your cover photo consists of a single image, it's vital that you are creative to maximize this important advertising medium. Collages can be useful. I suggest you create your cover image outside of Facebook by combining several shots of your business into a single image, then uploading this image. This will give you the ability to play around with the format, making changes until you are satisfied with its appearance.

While your cover photo can only be a single image, you can change it out as often as you like. This image is the first impression your target audience get of your business, so it is important to create a memorable impression. You want to use a photo that sums up what your business is about and what your brand represents. You may want to create several photos so that you'll have a replacement handy whenever you're ready for a change. On your cover photo, you'll also want to highlight any upcoming special events or deals you may have running. If you are a dress designer with a newly launched line of wedding dresses, you might display your latest designs in your cover photo.

Facebook has also made it possible for businesses to replace their cover photos with a *cover video*. A high-quality short video can boost your following and may keep you ahead of your competition. As with your cover photo, cover videos must be 820x312 pixels and they should be more than 20 seconds long but no longer than a minute and a half. Once you have uploaded your cover video, it automatically loops without sound and plays when anyone visits your business page. Visitors can turn on the sound by hovering over the video and clicking on it.

Profile Avatars

Your *profile picture* is the small icon that sits on the left of your cover photo. Whenever you write a comment, reply to a comment, or post on your timeline, a small copy of your profile picture will automatically show up.

This image is 170x170 pixels. You can upload a profile picture, by hovering your mouse over the frame of your profile picture (loaded on another site) and choose the option to "upload photo." Then pick your best image and download it to your business page. Even though you can only use a single image as a profile picture, you can update it whenever you feel necessary. You may want to establish a separate photo library where you can store extra cover and profile photos and change them whenever you want to.

I have always found it best to use a picture that is square-shaped; however, Facebook does give you the chance to crop your profile image out of whatever photo you decide to use. Although your profile picture is far smaller than your cover photo, it is still important to use a high-quality, professional photo that represents your business in the best light.

While most businesses choose to use a good picture of their company logo as their profile picture, some businesses will use a photo of a key product. A personal photo is rare, but it's useful if your business offers a service where you are the representative the customers will work with. If you run a personal tutoring service, you can defuse potential unease by providing a headshot to show your target audience who will be doing the tutoring.

Timeline Imagery

When it comes to displaying *images on your timeline*, there are several options available to you. Each single photo you upload onto your timeline will be compressed by Facebook to 476x714 pixels. This image will appear in preview mode; then, when someone clicks on the picture, they will then get to see the entire image.

If you choose to upload a group of several photos together, they will be displayed in the dimensions of the largest image. Vertical and horizontal photos will usually be loaded together. Since this is dependent on the shape and size, you may find that one will become the main image and be displayed as a larger snapshot than the rest.

If you want, you can let other users post their photos on your timeline. However, you do have the ability to prevent others from posting pictures on your page. To accomplish either permission to post or disallowing other users' photos, select settings, and set the box that enables the function.

Posting Links

If you choose to share a link via your timeline, simply paste the URL into the text box along with your personal message. A 476x249 pixel image related to the linked page will be displayed in a preview format. The name of the page connected to the link will also be shown under the preview picture with a brief description of the page. Once this thumbnail image and description appears, you can delete the URL you pasted.

Using Videos

Video is the most rapidly expanding area of Facebook. This medium provides the perfect showcase for any type of business. Statistics show that videos hold the attention longer than static images, so if you have a choice, use a video instead of a still shot.

It is as easy to upload videos to your business pages as still images. It is possible to load your videos onto outside video hosting sites – such as YouTube – and then link to them, but your business will not reap the benefits of engagement that are available when you upload directly to Facebook, so why would you bother to do that? If you've grabbed your audience's attention in a Facebook video, it's a simple matter to direct viewer traffic toward your website for more in-depth information, to engage with you directly, or better yet, to provide an opportunity to make a purchase.

You'll want to center your video on a topic that is trending and try to engage with the minds of your audience. At the end of your video, invite interaction by encouraging the viewer to like or share it.

A recent Nielson study reported that most of our recall of advertising occurs within the first ten seconds. Therefore, instead of uploading an exhaustive video, you would be better served to use a short video clip to capture the imagination of your audience and then invite them to learn more by clicking a link to your website.

Now for the technical details. When recording videos to post on Facebook, the optimum resolution size is 720p. Even though you can upload videos in any digital format, the best are .mov or.mp4, since these formats prefer quality over compression.

While it is important for your video to have superior sound quality, it is even more essential for your video to be interesting without sound. A running transcription allows people to get your message, even if they don't have the ability to hear the audio portion of your recording.

You'll want to capture and focus viewers' attention immediately, during the first few seconds of play. Keep in mind that your videos will be running without sound until the user clicks on the image to activate the audio. It's important to start the video with something that will pique curiosity or entice the viewer to want to watch more.

For the same reason you will need to carefully select the thumbnail image that represents your video. You can choose this by hovering your mouse over your video and choosing the appropriate options on the pop-up menu.

Go Live

Facebook Live enables users to live stream video to their audience, essentially bringing them into the moment with you. Research has revealed that people are three times more likely to watch a live streaming video than something pre-recorded. Businesses can utilize live streaming to include an audience in the broadcast of their special events, product launches, and slice-of-life postings.

Extended Length Videos

Apart from Facebook live, you also have the option to upload prerecorded videos that are more than 20 minutes long, or mini-movies. Most of the time, you'll want to keep your videos short and concise, three minutes at the most but sometimes the situation may call for a longer presentation. If you're publishing an extended lecture, a webinar, or a long musical performance, however, you'll need a longer video.

Promoting Your Videos

As soon as you have uploaded your video to your business page, it's time to start targeting your audience. Just look for the "Boost Post" button that will be located under your published video. When you click on the button it will take you to an additional page where you can select where your Facebook business page is shown and then target it toward a specific audience. This feature allows you to target specific countries and states and select how many days the video will appear, for up to two weeks.

Auto-Play

I typically prefer to use the auto-play feature. When you upload your videos directly to your Facebook business page, they will appear on a user's timeline and begin playing automatically. Videos uploaded using a third-party link will not. If most of your business videos are hosted on a different video site, you will still be able to upload them to Facebook, but you will only want to upload the ones that work best with Facebook. In other words, only use videos that are short and relevant. If necessary, you might also consider editing your video, shortening it to a length that is more appropriate for Facebook. You have the option then to add a message to the end of the video directing the viewers to the longer version; this will also mean more traffic through your social media outlets.

When you upload your videos directly to Facebook, you have the option of embedding their links in other locations, such as your blog or website. By doing this, your videos will grab more views and thereby boost interaction on your business page. Embedding a Facebook video in your blog or website is easy to do; just click the arrow you see in the upper right corner of your video and choose "embed." This will generate a box with a code. You then need to paste this code to your website or blog and publish it. This video will then appear automatically whenever anyone views your blog or website.

The Playlist

After you have uploaded a suitable number of videos to your business page, you will want to organize them into a playlist. This makes it easy for your audience to identify the videos they intend to view.

Creating a playlist is a straightforward process. Simply go to the video manager and use the option to create a playlist. When you have chosen this option, a box will pop up and you can create a unique name for the playlist and a brief description. Click "next" and Facebook will open a window that allows you to select videos for inclusion in your playlist. Click next and your playlist is ready for use.

Diversify Your Content

People like Facebook business pages because they can stay informed easily. Rather than posting the same type of content each day, your business page will be more interesting to your audience if change things up. Post something completely different to keep the attention of your followers. Remember, people take in information in diverse ways. Some people prefer to read the information while others are more visual and would rather learn things by watching a video. I have found that mixing text posts with other content, such as videos and still images, has proven the best way to engage with my audience. I also throw in a trivia quiz every now and then to tempt my audience to interact, not only with me but also with each other as well.

Ask Questions

If you do it right, asking questions of your audience can open a firestorm of participation. In addition to boosting audience loyalty, you can use questions to gather information for demographic research. Or, you can issue your query just for the fun of it.

If you decide to ask a question to stimulate audience participation, you'll want to word it so that the answer can be kept to a single word or phrase. Anything longer takes the fun out of the game.

People love to talk about themselves, so you will see the most interaction if you ask your audience to share their opinion or state their preference. You can even ask your audience to help make a minor business decision, like choosing the name of an upcoming product.

Use your audience's responses as an opportunity to interact with people outside of your product-related business. This will humanize your business, making it more attractive to your potential customers. People always prefer doing business with a friend than with a stranger; anything you can do to build a person-to-person connection with your audience will always be to your advantage.

Post Boldly

Do not hesitate to post content that other businesses avoid. By this I don't mean anything offensive or obnoxious, just something that is totally different from the norm. You want to provoke thought and responses without offending, if possible. You will generally receive a huge positive response to this content, because people like to be surprised by something unique.

Even if a post is met with negative responses, learn from them, apologize to those who are offended, and move on to something else. There's nothing wrong with shaping your content according to what is trending. It makes sense to choose topics that people already have on their minds. But you'll want to try to find a unique angle; don't just parrot what others are saying, but boldly stick out your neck and say what you truly think. You usually won't get your head chopped off, but even if you do, you will have stimulated a response and encouraged interaction with and between your followers. Most people have strong opinions when it comes to trending topics and they are more likely to share their opinions and get involved if you give them an opportunity to discuss the topic further.

Plan Your Posts

Personally, I have found the most effective strategy for posting a good mix of content involves using a calendar to plan out my posts ahead of time. That way, I can ensure a healthy variety in my postings. I can balance more intense topics with lighter content and sprinkle in a good dose of humor to even out the mix.

The calendar allows you to also take full advantage of what is trending to engage with your audience around seasonal topics. Posting content relevant to Christmas at the beginning of December is one example. You can tie the needs of the season to your products, with special offers to celebrate appropriate holidays and national days and sales to punctuate tax season or other days that have special significance.

Chapter 14 Psychology Behind Ads

5 Ps of the Marketing & Other Elements

There're so many reasons people buy, reasons which are referred to in the marketing books as 5 Ps. The 5 Ps are people, product, promotion, price, and placement. When used correctly, these five Ps could push the customers to convert right away.

Product

Customers would buy from you is you give a superior service or product which meets their requirements. When this comes to the Facebook ads, you have to show your customers that the service or product is far better as compared to your competitors'.

Price

The customers would buy from you when the product or service is fairly charged.

Placement

It is one more element which compels the customers to purchase is placement or a location of the product. Strategic placement of the Facebook ads is the main key. You might create your store location ad to target audience within the store location.

Facebook Ad Placement
Promotion

It could quickly urge customers to buy your offer. Promotions are temporary deals which cause your customers to quickly buy. Offering some promotion might often be some kind of strong tactic for driving customers to buy your product.

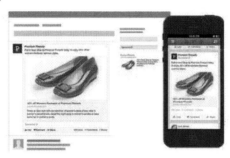

Social Proof
People

The 5th P that is people pertains to public figures' and friends' influence on somebody's purchasing decision. Experts say that the customers are going to buy a product if this has been praised or recommended by a celebrity, friends, a public figure, or family.

Including social proof is a vital strategy. Although there're many ways that you could include social proof, just like partnering with the influencers or adding your customer reviews to the ad creatives.

Evoking Emotions

When there is one thing that is true regarding humans, it is that they're impatient. When people are impatient in their routine lives then you could think how impatient they're while browsing the web. Especially, on Facebook, every second does matter. You might stop customers mid scroll by making high-quality, eye-catching creatives & compelling copies. So, you can maintain customers' attention by making an ad which evokes their emotions, spurring to buy.

Urgency

To create urgency is the best way to compel users to complete the desired action. Rather, usually successful ad campaigns announce "24-hour sale" & "this deal will expire at midnight."

Urgency Ad
Scarcity

If people think that this particular product is actually in low supply then they want to take an action as they fear the loss of that item. Often, scarcity tactics work well along with discounts or sales that give the advantage of purchasing the product.

Difficulty

In order to alleviate customers' skepticism, you'll have to give away some free items. Try giving free items as the customers have followed or liked your Facebook page, left a good review about the business, or take a short survey. If you use us free items as the incentives, you are giving a realistic offer which would allay doubts.

Kinship

Customers would give a response to your ads because they accept those people who are just like them. You need to be more relatable to the customers and try to speak their language. It means that you need to speak as a 21-year-old lady. This way, your ad would be much impactful.

Psychological Impact of Different Colors

It is highly unlikely you will pay attention to an ad's colors. A color, as this turns out, actually evokes customers' feelings as well as tones which can influence the audience's psychology. Look at the following chart that contains different effects of the colors.

Best Creative Practices: Image, Copy, and Video

Your design of an ad is very important so you should learn how to make your Facebook ad without teaching you about how to make them well. So, in this section, I will give you some important tips on how you can improve the ad creatives.

Copy

It consists of the heart of a message. It depends what your ad is all about & what you actually want your customers to do just after viewing your ad. A good copy might contribute to your ad's success—this does matter.

The ad copies would appear in 3 areas of an ad: a description under its headline, a text above its image, and a headline under its image. It is good to know about the text specifications for these 3 areas. Following are Facebook's ads copy essentials

Format: Slideshows, Videos, and Single Images

Text: Characters must be 125. Text more than 125 characters is although allowed but might be truncated.

Link description: Characters must be 30. Text more than 30 is also allowed but might be truncated.

Headline: Characters must be 25. Text more than 25 characters is also allowed but might be truncated.

Text: Characters must be 90. You can text more than 90 characters but might be truncated.

Headline: Characters must be 25. You can text more than 25 characters but might be truncated. The *Format is Carousel.*

Text: Characters must be 125. You can text more than 125 characters but might be truncated.

Headline: Characters must be 40. You can text more than 40 characters but might be truncated.

Link description: Characters must be 20. You can text more than 20 but might be truncated.

The Format is Dynamic Product Ads - could be carousel or single image

Text: Characters must be 255.

Use Before & After Effect

To make your copies more effective, you need to make sure that they are compelling and relevant & that they give a nice solution to your issue. See before-&-after chart given below. The copy must illustrate your audience's state before your service or product & after your service or product.

Know the Target Audience

While you are creating your copies, you should know your target audience. You must know how a person thinks, know who you are writing for, & know what a person wants. For knowing your audience, you need to make some fictional character or a persona who actually possesses similar needs, demographics, lifestyles, and behaviors, and attitudes according to your customers.

Do not be much Salesy

The copy shouldn't sound much salesy. Keep in mind that the audience is also on social media for socializing with their peers than to purchase your products. As your customers have no buying intent so they can feel annoyed due to the ads. The ads should take a mild selling approach. So, instead of pushing your sale, you should give an idea & offer a suitable solution to an issue which shows your customers what life will be by using that product, use before-&-after effect.

Reuse those Headline Formats which Work

In case specific headline formats have worked historically for you, do not hesitate to reusing those.

Images

The ad's images are the most crucial and most dominant element of the ad as, because of its big size, it is the very first thing that users view. Unluckily, an image has some seconds to take the users' attention quickly scrolling via their feeds. In order to stop mid scrolling, you must use your images with the attractive colors which are vibrant & also contrast against the elements within your ads or against News Feed.

Objects and People

You've to try several kinds of images that include images featuring objects or people. Research has shown that the images with recognizable and relatable people do better than those images without any recognizable people. Hence, this tactic is very famous that several brands try to hire popular celebrities who could sponsor products.

Also, you can add some credibility to the ads by featuring the symbols, logos, and objects of recognized companies. So, add them in the ad in case your service or product integrates with the brands.

When you select feature objects instead of people in the Facebook ad then go a step ahead & feature your product. Doing so would get 2 things. One, in case the featured product is attractive in that image then people would click on that ad. Two, in case you feature a product in your ad then people can imagine themselves with that product.

Include the 3 *E*s

The 3 Es are very important for the performance of your ad.

Entertainment

For catching people's attention, the ads must fulfill their requirements to be entertained. You need to make sure that your ad makes people cry, smile, or laugh.

Educate

The educational content would cause a curious & knowledge-hungry audience to pause mid-scroll. You must create content which educates your users about the products & shows how your services or products are great solutions.

Engage

Posts having much engagement would show higher on the news feed rather than posts which have less engagement. It means that you have to create irresistible an ad which your audience could not assist but engage with it.

Video

Videos work exceptionally with your storytelling. And, with this form of the moving creative, audience would watch your story whether the story is regarding your product, service, or brand.

4 Tips to Keep in Mind

There're 4 things that you must do while creating your video ads. One, you need to keep in mind that it is short that is with the length of at least 1 minute. Two, place your story's crucial message within the starting of your ad. Three, you must always make your sound off video as most people watch it without sound. Four, you need to make sure the video's story is comprehensible without sound or captions.

Video Ads Specs

Surely, all your videos have to follow Facebook's ad specs. Or, they will appear quite strangely on the ad—& you do not want that.

Practices for the Instagram Stories

When you have to put your video to the Instagram Stories then make sure that your video works great for the Instagram Stories users. Following are top 5 suggestions about your Instagram Stories.

1. Keep Your Video Short

Instagram Stories users are more impatient. You need to keep the video length about 15 seconds.

2. Make Your Video Relevant

While creating Instagram Stories ads, you must make sure your content is always relatable to your audience.

3. Make for the Sound Off, Delightful with the Sound

You should use delight music which people would enjoy. However, if somebody decides not to see Stories with the sound then it is important to design the sound off Stories.

4. Use Quick Videos

In case your Stories ads contain more than 1 clip or scene then edit your clips together in order to make the fast-paced video.

5. Creative Tools of Instagram

With the passage of time, Instagram rolled out important tools that let people beautify and decorate their mundane Stories. Following are Instagram tools that you might use.

- Color: alters your text color

- Pens: you'll write and draw on the Story by using 3 different pens: chalk, sharpie, eraser, highlighter, and neon

- Gifs: you might beautify a Story with the gifs

- Superzoom: you could zoom in to the object with 3 sound effects

- Rewind: You can record the actions backward

- Text: You can include text to the Story

- Color picker: It picks out one color from the Story & imitates this hence you could use a new colour for the pens and text

- Emojis: put emojis in your Story

- Stickers: You can use static and moving stickers

- Mention: mention other accounts

- Boomerang: It takes the looping stop-motion videos

Chapter 15 AdWords vs. Facebook

This is a question that often inexperienced marketers ask. The answer is always "it depends".

We need to understand what are the goals that we want to achieve with our advertising campaign. It is often fundamental to combine both strategies. It all depends on the type of question: whether this is latent or conscious (or both).

If the goal is to make branding and then stimulate users who do not know us and may be interested (latent demand), the best choice is Facebook Ads, which will allow you, as we will see later, to reach potential customers. You can do this with various types of targeted campaigns and get leads.

Similarly, you can also take advantage of ads on the Google Display Network to reach potential customers by submitting your banners to specific placements.

If users are already looking for your product or service, the right approach is to use Google AdWords by creating ads on the Search Network. In this case, the user is already in a much lower part of the funnel, therefore more inclined to purchase as the user is looking for your product/service.

Obviously, in most cases, we will find both types of demand and we will have to work on both platforms jointly.

The key is to understand where the user is inside our sales funnel and act accordingly; we will never tire of stressing it.

Going inside, it will be useful to retarget users who have shown interest in the product or service working with both Facebook Ads and AdWords through ads on the display network.

What if we intercept potential customers on Facebook through FB Ads and these, then, look for us on Google but we are not positioned in an organic way (without paying) for that keyword?

Simple. They will click on a competition link. The risk is, therefore, to practically advertise competitors. Understand well then how important it is, in the absence of organic positioning with SEO, that we must also have Google ads on the search network to cover some keywords as well.

Facebook marketing is not so powerful if done alone; it is something that some people see as a disadvantage.

Each Facebook campaign consists of 3 levels and it starts from the campaign level, which consists of one or more ad groups.

As you have just read, for each campaign you create, you will have to choose a goal. This is the real distinctive factor at the campaign level.

At the Ad Group level (Ad Set), you will have to choose the target, the available budget, the publication times, the offer, and the placements.

Going down the hierarchy, at the level of the announcements, you can set the type of announcement (image, video, carousel, etc.), all the texts, the call to action (action button), and the destination links.

As mentioned, the structure is hierarchical, so if you pause (or delete) for example a group of ads, the same thing will happen to all ads below that group.

The Definition of the Goals

Now that we understand the structure of a Facebook campaign and what are the parameters to be set for each level, we are ready to launch our first campaign.

The first question is: "What is the goal to be achieved?"

Do you want to sell a certain product because maybe you have an e-commerce store? Do you want to create awareness or reputation? Do you want to have leads?

Often, in a complete web marketing strategy, we will have to create different campaigns for the different phases of the purchasing process. We can then create different ads depending on whether the target user does not know our brand or knows it but does not know our product/service, or, for example, knows our product/service and may be interested in a commercial offer.

Facebook itself in the creation phase will propose you different objectives divided into 4 macro-categories. Let's see them in detail one by one.

- ***Brand Awareness***

When to use it: in large-scale campaigns, when there is not a particular action that you want to take to the user. This goal will be more attractive to large companies that can afford to launch campaigns for pure branding. For smaller companies, however, almost every other objective will give better and more significant results.

- ***Reach***

When to use it: similar to the brand awareness goal, the reach objective is functional to reach the maximum number of users to which the ad will show. With the introduction of the rules, Facebook now allows you to put a cap on the frequency with which the ad is shown to the same user; in this sense, the goal for reach becomes very useful when you have to work with a relatively small audience and you want everyone to view the ad.

- ### *Traffic*

When to use it: when we want to take users to a website, or on a landing page, for example. It is a very interesting goal when promoting content, such as a blog post.

- ### *Leads*

When to use it: the lead ads greatly simplify the signup process from mobile devices. When someone clicks on the ad, a form opens with all personal contact information already pre-filled based on the information they share on Facebook, such as name, surname, phone, and email address. This aspect makes the process really fast and within 2 clicks, one to open the ad and one to send the information.

The only problem with this type of objective is that, often, the email address used to sign up for Facebook several years ago is obsolete and has not been updated for too long. In this case, we would get a useless contact. As a result, it has been seen that better conversion campaigns perform that point to specific external landing pages with data to be filled out.

Another aspect to keep in mind is that lead ads do not allow you to include all the information you want in the offer, like on a landing page. Therefore, for campaigns that require a great deal of cognitive attention from the user, a campaign for conversions will be more successful.

That said, in any case, it is always better to do a test between the two approaches and see which performs better, because each case and sector can behave differently.

The success of a Facebook campaign depends almost entirely on how we select the right target. Good results are not obtained by trying to guess the interests, but only by experimenting and testing, and knowing the right tools.

The Pixel of Facebook

James Fend, a Facebook expert, is categorical: the pixel of Facebook should always be installed anyway, even if at the moment, we are not interested in campaigning and even if we believe we do not need anything. But why? Because when it is installed (by entering a code on our website), it starts recording data. The pixel will then be able to make us reach users who come into contact with our site, and these users can be used in future for our listings. It must be installed "regardless" because we may regret not having collected the data when these will help us.

Spy on Competitors' Sponsorships

Coming into an advertisement published by our competitors can be a golden opportunity: we can "spy" the target they have chosen for their sponsorship. Just click on "Why do I view this ad?", where the magic is accomplished: we will see exactly what target has set our competitor.

If the interests that our competitor has selected work we do not know, we can get an idea based on the vanity metrics. And in any case, we now have some tools to test.

Create a Personalized Audience

Facebook gives us many options to intercept our potential customers and we should always start from our customers or our traffic. For example, we can upload a file with our LinkedIn contacts or newsletter subscribers. We can take advantage of the pixel and select who visits specific pages of the site or generate events (such as sales or add to cart), who spends more time on the site or who visit him more often, or who opens the newsletter.

Take Advantage of Other Channels, like AdWords

The ads on Facebook certainly do not answer to any conscious question: we launch the bait to a potentially interested public and hope that someone will realize that they need our product or service. With ads on

AdWords instead, we intercept the conscious need: the user need the tires and search on Google, find our ad, and land on our site.

Well, we can take advantage of the results obtained from AdWords. Such as? Just leave the pixel of Facebook "listening" and with the data obtained create our custom audience based on traffic on the site.

At that point the user, who has seen our model X of tires but who has not completed the purchase, will see "chased" from our product even within Facebook.

Use A/B Testing

The analysis of the results obtained must always be exploited to our advantage. Facebook gives us the opportunity with A/B testing.

Facebook Campaigns: Rules to Define the Budget

The risk of wasting money on Facebook campaigns is very high. To avoid spending money badly, there are a series of precautions that is best to undertake.

Rules to improve CPAs (cost per action) by working on the budget:

Do not choose too ambitious self-optimization goals. This is especially true for e-commerce, but it is always applicable: it takes an amount of daily conversions high enough for campaigns to be able to learn effectively and improve their performance. We use micro-conversions, i.e. intermediate conversions that are easier to obtain.

Head different configurations. When the available budget allows it and "we are allowed to make mistakes", it is good to test different configurations in order to find the ideal setting.

Increase the budget progressively. When a campaign proves to be performing it is normal to want to increase the budget allocated to it and make it climb. However, the increase must be progressive and for small steps (10%-20%). Or, if there is urgency, better clone the campaign and create a new one with the desired budget. Otherwise, 9/10, there is an increase in CPC and a general decline in performance.

Do not accept default placements. Always separate positions in groups with the same target until proven otherwise.

Conclusion

Thank you again for downloading this book!

I hope I was able to help you reach your marketing goals using Facebook.

As you have seen, this form of marketing allows opportunities traditionally beyond the reach of regular advertising. Hopefully, you have learned one of two things; either how to grow your Facebook page and successfully promote your own business on the website or how to cash in on your success and turn your followership into a source of passive income as well, wherever that audience may be gathered on the internet.

The best thing about Facebook and the Internet, in general, is the fact that most business ventures you want to try yourself in require little to no financial investment, especially in the beginning. And as the internet and social media engrave themselves even deeper into our everyday lives and develop even further in the future, these opportunities are bound to become only more accessible to all.

The vast majority of users on the website use Facebook every day without even thinking about the business potential that's right in front of them the whole time. But, those who run a business have generally realized the importance of social media, and you will find that even the smallest of businesses have their Facebook pages nowadays. While it's true that a lot of those pages don't grow that much, this is not something that's beyond their control. The difference between them and you is that they are not well-informed, unfortunately, and simply lack the knowhow to take their page to new heights. Hopefully, now you possess enough of that information to make yourself stand out from the crowd.

The next step is to continue to create and share content that your followers love and to build relationships that may convert to future sales.

Keep this book handy when implementing your Facebook marketing strategies and come back to it every time you feel a little lost in the Facebook marketing world.

Remember to keep evolving your relationship with your customers and followers and remain in touch with their requirements and interests. A business that cherishes their relationship with the clients is the healthiest and most solid in the long run, and Facebook has facilitated the building of such a relationship like no platform has done ever before.

If we continue down this road, then perhaps television and print will continue to decline in popularity, if not become completely pushed aside by the internet and social media. We could very well be on the ground floor of something completely new. We could see a time when social media becomes so prevalent throughout the world that the very concept of media changes dramatically and evolves into something else entirely.

Think back to a time when television was just starting to become more popular and accessible for a moment. Television forever revolutionized media, but at first, it gave a voice only to a select few people, like the state or big businesses and those who they would give the floor to from time to time. Nowadays, with social media, virtually anybody with an internet connection has the potential to reach millions, if not billions of people throughout the world. This allows us to share ideas and advanced knowledge with such ease, let alone share and promote a line of products or a service. Influence and power are now measured by views, followers, and visitor traffic. Even if an audience is all you have going for your page, once you achieve a large one, you will instantly be faced with numerous opportunities and new roads to take, letting you choose the direction you want to take with your business.

Made in the USA
Middletown, DE
26 August 2020